Five Ways to Create Peace in the Middle East

Bruce Masters

Copyright information

Copyright 2024 Bruce Masters. All rights reserved.

Independently Published. ISBN: 9798345192030

First Edition – UK English.

brucemasters.org

Introduction

This guide to achieving peace between Arabs and Jews, between Islam and Judaism and between the Jewish and Palestinian peoples will increase empathy and understanding, remove the propaganda and rhetoric, which is a barrier to ensuring both the Palestinian and Israeli people are protected and safeguarded, whilst guarding against a catastrophic escalation of the initial conflict, which will be certain to result in millions of lives lost.

Each plan suggested within these pages is the product not of emotion, not of being moved by emotive imagery or suffering from either side, but of a desire to end all bloodshed, to restore good order and to get all people in the region back to work, back to school, back to a peaceful and harmonious home life; back to normalcy.

Each of these plans will halt the rocket attacks, halt the kidnappings, halt the construction of new tunnels, halt Israeli backlashes and incursions into Palestine and halt the destabilising and devastating long-term harm caused by these two neighbors battling it out in heavily urbanized areas, which guarantees the continuation of civilian casualties. All sides must agree that protecting civilians must be our first priority when conceiving and implementing long-term fixes in the region. Change is needed, huge change, the kind of change found within these five plans.

If the Saudi Proposal is chosen as a preference, if the Donbas 'no man's land' plan is chosen, if the 'Iranian Resettlement Plan' is chosen or if the United States of Israel plan is chosen, real fundamental change will be ushered in, which is what all peoples and states in the region require in order to break the deadlock and stalemates.

In order to save all civilians from coming to further harm, kidnappings, slaughter or bombings, dramatic change is necessary in order to birth a fresh, optimistic and peaceful new start.

It is hard not to sympathize with Palestinian civilians who are caught up in the regional clashes and oftentimes our feelings of compassion for the innocents of Palestine and the civilians found therein, who for the longest time have lived in limbo, an unenviable existence resplendent with fear, turn into anger and hatred for the powerful state of Israel. Yet, believe me when I tell you that the anger you may feel towards Israel today if, for instance, you live in the West, if you attend every pro-Palestine demonstration possible, will be completely gone, nullified, but a memory once one of these means to create eternal peace in the Middle East is enacted.

Do not think cynically that the hatred will be there for good; do not believe the Middle East fated to eternally war and for you to eternally be forced to honourably take the side of the apparent underdog, as peace is certainly on the horizon.

Gone be the pessimism and cynicism; gone be the hate and immersion in foreign suffering, which creates little more than numbness and compassion fatigue and bitter angst.

There exists an opportunity in this hour to save Gaza, to save Palestinians, to save Israel, to start again, to create awesome rejuvenating peace.

I know you desire peace, I desire peace, the average Israeli and average Palestinian desires peace, because we are all humans and the fight for peace, mutual respect and brotherhood is our shared collective fight. It unites us in common purpose.

Thanks for Your Time

Hello, I just wanted to thank you in advance for your time.

I hope there is something positive, entertaining and useful in each of my books for everyone.

If you would like to reproduce any of my books for any reason, in any language or format, please feel free to do so for journalism, education or business purposes—if you can profit from my words, please do so, I will never request royalties.

If you enjoy this book, find it helpful, interesting or educational, please share a copy with a friend or tell others about these books and consider leaving a review or some feedback, which would be much appreciated.

Thanks again for your time. It is very nice to meet you.

Bruce

Contents

Copyright information ii

Introduction iii

Thanks for Your Time...v

Contents...vi

Chapter One — Why No White Flag? 1

Chapter Two — Honesty and Reality..5

Chapter Three — Background, Impartiality and Fiery Optimism 8

Chapter Four — Two Important Questions and an Important Point.........12

Chapter Five — Extremism, "Terrorists" and Dresden.........................16

Chapter Six — The Saudi Proposal..18

Chapter Seven — The Donbas 'No Man's Land' Peace Plan....................26

Chapter Eight — The Iranian Resettlement Plan.................................34

Chapter Nine — The United States of Israel 37

Chapter Ten — Plan C..40

Chapter Eleven — The 51st and 52nd States of America.......................41

Chapter Twelve — Pour Nuclear Waste into Nuclear Bunkers—It's Meant to Be 48

Chapter Thirteen — The Chief Negotiator...51

Chapter Fourteen — The UN, NGOs and Foreign Aid........................53

Chapter Fifteen — Delyo Is ALL OF US 56

Conclusion...60

The Peace Series...68

About the Author..70

Books by the Author 71

Chapter One — Why No White Flag?

Why has Hamas not yet surrendered?

Why have Gazans/Palestinians not surrendered and raised white flags when the Germans, as powerful as they were in 1945, surrendered and agreed to occupation from multiple nations and armies? Why is it that there has been no surrender despite knowing, just as Japan and Germany knew in 1945 (which is why they surrendered), that victory, an absolute victory over their competitor is impossible?

This is an important question, one that needs to be asked and discussed, because the surrender would cause every militant and fighter and tunnel-digger to be forced to either vacate Palestine or to immediately change, mend their ways and embrace peace, dialogue and democracy—as the remnants of the SS and Gestapo were grudgingly forced to do.

Many Israeli hostages still being held in the tunnel networks, with some perhaps also having been relocated to neighbouring states, proves the white flag has not been raised, that surrender has not been signalled. Until the last hostage is released, the defiance and conflict continue.

Not surrendering communicates strange and mixed messages to the West as well as to other parts of the world, which is in large part why so many folk, especially those who identify as liberal and woke, take the side of the apparent underdog in the conflict, the Palestinians. Yet, are they independent and on their own and sovereign or are they little more than unfortunate pawns caught up in a much larger conflict? It seems to me they are sacrifices who deserve better, who can and should walk away from violence and conflict as soon possible, before the New Year if possible in fact, thanks to one of the peace proposals introduced later in this book.

So why is it there is no surrender when we consider that the proud Germans and proud Japanese surrendered, when we consider also that the proud folk of Jersey and Guernsey surrendered to the invading German forces in WWII and lived under occupation peacefully throughout the war?

Why is it that, despite being defeated by their competitor (Israel) and unable to defend themselves, let alone inflict substantial harm upon their foe, they refuse to wave the white flag as the Germans have in the past, as the Japanese have, as the Brits and the French have, as the Ottoman

Empire once did also in order to prevent unnecessary bloodshed and civilian casualties, why? Why?

The answer is simple, and obvious, and you will agree with this assessment irrespective of your current position on the ongoing but soon-to-be-brought-to-a-crashing-halt conflict between Israel and Palestine, which, in truth, is a conflict between Israel and the entire Middle East.

It does not benefit Israel in any way to have conflicts with Palestinians, it is terrible PR; it creates new enemies in the future when the sons of slain fighters grow up and demand justice and retribution. It is a terrible thing for Israel in all ways for the conflict to continue, so please understand that Israel does not want to fight against Palestine or Palestinians; there is no deep hatred there as Israel can and will defend herself and Palestine does not pose an existential threat to the existence of the state of Israel.

But it does benefit other states in the region when Israel battles with militants and folk she refers to as terrorists, who are called "freedom fighters" by some in the West, and that is the crux of the issue.

Imagine, for a moment, that the only Arab Muslims in the Middle East were the few million folk residing in the territory of Palestine, that every Muslim nation and every Arab nation was solely inhabited by Buddhists or Hindus or Christians in 2024 who took a neutral position on the conflict between Israel and Palestine.

Tell me, honestly, do you think that in that eventuality, if there were no other Muslim states and no other Arab nations in the region, the October 7th atrocity would have occurred?

The answer, you know and I know, is no.

Beyond the foreign funding for that audacious attack, which precipitated the destruction of multiple Palestinian towns and cities and the loss of so much life and peace, as Israeli hostages still languish in tunnels under the earth, holding on to the hope that they will once again be free, the existence of "supportive" and "encouraging" and "backing" Arab and Muslim states in the region is the sole reason the attack occurred.

If Hamas and the Palestinian people were on their own, no foreign supporters, no foreign backers, no NGOs assisting them, no UN support, all on their own, it would be the height of madness, absolute suicide, for the entire nation and people to send a handful of paragliders against a nuclear power!

If every other nation in the region were gone, gone would be Hamas and Hezbollah. It is quite simple really. This is why there has been no surrender; this is why there has been no white flag raised as is normally the case because Palestine is not sovereign. Rather, the innocent Palestinian people are being used to engage in a proxy war against Israel to weaken and destabilise her and her democracy, this proxy war being fuelled by states in the Middle East, foreign aid, NGOs and radicals within the UN.

The "fight for Palestinian Freedom" is in fact the "fight to eradicate the state of Israel" with Palestinians being wilfully sacrificed, marched to the front of an unwinnable war by foreign leftists and western neo-Marxists, by Muslim Arab "allies" and by every man and woman across the world who does not know enough about the conflict to be able to opine yet who understandably sees the Palestinians as being the virtuous hard-done-by underdog. This is why so much money and so many resources flood into Gaza, with so much of it being used to acquire more rockets, more bullets and more shovels to dig ever more tunnels under the ground to house even more kidnapped innocent Israelis.

The folk in Jersey, strong Britons, raised the white flag when the SS landed. Why? Because they were not suicidal, not stupid, and were not lost to cultish brainwashing; nor did they viscerally on a cellular level hate the German race—despite only a few decades prior fighting to the death against their European cousins in the fields of Flanders and the Somme.

The refusal to surrender to an unbeatable opponent (as Israel is) seems to be suggestive of heroism, or righteousness, or virtue, or passion for a cause or justice; yet it is none of these things because if you were to click your fingers and every Arab and Muslim nation other than Palestine were suddenly, miraculously depopulated completely, every Palestinian woman and child and civilian would be forced to demand new elections, demand democracy, demand their leaders build schools rather than terror tunnels and immediately white flags would be raised everywhere because the Palestinian people wish to live. They wish to live long rewarding amazing lives, they wish to preserve their culture and traditions and blood, which are all threatened when you poke a ferocious lion and steal his cubs.

The solution is not to destroy that which is outside, which causes the internal conflict in Palestine and Israel to continue unendingly; no, we are not yet at the stage of bleakness, abject cynicism and genocide. Rather, the five solutions offered within the pages of this unexpected and thought-provoking and certifiably peace-multiplying book are those that are desperately needed in this hour.

If you find fault with aspects of any of these plans, please fix that fault or proffer a superior universally amicable solution. But if no fault or criticism is possible and one of these five suggestions is accepted by all sides directly involved in a last-ditch attempt to stave off a repeat of the Six-Day War in 1967 but on a far greater and more devastating scale than most could imagine, please embrace peace, radical and unapologetic peace. It will ruffle feathers and cannot make every man on the planet ecstatic; yet, it will ensure Palestine and her people survive and thrive and will safeguard the Jewish people and the Jewish state forevermore.

Chapter Two — Honesty and Reality

Gaza and the Palestinian territories would exponentially grow in size if Israel and Lebanon were suddenly abandoned by their respective populations.

It is a myth, childish thinking, to believe any state, any people, would not immediately take advantage and seize the opportunity to double, triple or quadruple the size of their domain.

Chinatowns only remain the same size due to being surrounded; remove the folk surrounding Chinatowns and they will massively increase in size, of course.

Empty Lebanon, what happens next? The Palestinian flag is raised there.

Empty half of Saudi Arabia, what happens next? The Palestinian flag is raised there.

The Palestinians being comparative underdogs to the Jews and the state of Israel is meaningless; the ambition there is of course not only to create full autonomy and self-governance but afterwards to expand wherever possible in all directions at once, which would be aided massively by underground networks of tunnels. If any nation discovers such 'terror tunnels' (terror because they are used to house kidnapped civilians and to transport weapons from A to B) located near to their borders, the reaction will always be identical to those of recent actions in Gaza as no nation or leader can ever sit idly by whilst those who wish to exterminate your state and your entire tribe plot, plan, expand and grow stronger subterraneously, ready to pop up out of holes in the ground, like gun-toting, cultishly radicalized moles, intent on destroying civilisation, democracy, peace and harmony.

Imagine in this very moment that the next time you click your fingers, every Israeli soldier, police officer, member of the military, Mossad agent and politician will be transported to the USA and forcibly kept there for the remainder of their lives, leaving behind only civilians in Israel, just civilians.

Do it now. Click your fingers and tell me do you believe that those who you may believe are "freedom fighters" would put away their weapons, fill in the terror tunnels, refrain from anymore bombings, killings, suicide attacks, and mass kidnappings and never again attack musical festivals where young folk are desperately seeking escapism from the horrific reality of living in a warzone due to a minority desiring undemocratic power and control and seeking to commit genocide against the ancient Jewish tribe, which gave rise to all Abrahamic monotheistic religions, including Islam?

After clicking your fingers, do you see those in the tunnels, those building rockets, which they know will strike civilians for a near certainty, who call for the death of the state of Israel habitually suddenly becoming passive, laissez faire, woke, liberal and internationalists committed to democracy who would go out of their way to ensure that every innocent Israeli citizen (whose ancestors, going back thousands of years are buried beneath Jerusalem) is protected, respected, loved, nurtured and permitted to remain alive and free?

If you believe this, you are a child or cultishly brainwashed. That is the Disney fantasy reality; that is the false populist narrative—that all Jews are evil and domineering whilst all Palestinians are good and merely desiring to be protected from external tribes and states.

Imagine if on that tragic day, October 7th, after invading Israel, after kidnapping defenseless men and women, boys and girls and pensioners and after murdering so many Israelis, the attackers had seen that the Israeli military, the IDF, and Mossad had not come out in force to meet the invader, to fight the invader and attempt to destroy the invader, following the invader to his homeland if necessary to get justice and to recover his family members, friends and cousins stolen away in such a barbaric and desperate and inciting manner.

Imagine that. Imagine if Israel had not responded to the initial incursion. Why would the attackers have fled with but a few hundred hostages and why would they be content to kill the limited number of Jews that they killed?

If there were no tanks on the way, no attack helicopters on the way, no IDF on the way, no jet fighters on the way, and no missiles and drones on the way, of course, for an absolute certainty, the attack would have continued. It would have become genocidal within mere days; every settlement would have been pillaged, every town sacked, every civilian rounded up and exiled to terror tunnels under Gaza. It is only due to the existence of strong defences and a military willing to fight and die at the drop of a hat that ensured October 7th did not result in one million Israeli casualties, or two, or even six.

Understand, when you kill one innocent in cold blood, when you kill a child dancing at a party, there is nothing to stop such a broken and sociopathic killing machine driven by pure hatred of the neighbouring tribe to go on killing and killing and killing forever, until that person is fought against, until their ideology and organisation is fought against and ultimately defeated and a new, unbeatable authority established to guard against any future attacks, incursions, invasions or mass kidnap and murder plots.

Chapter Three — Background, Impartiality and Fiery Optimism

It is important to say at this point that I am a huge optimist, not because I am naïve or gullible but rather because the Pyramids exist, because Stonehenge exists, because the Golden Gate Bridge exists and because humanity has defied the odds and nature and all else to triumphantly be still standing in 2024 as pandemics and extreme weather and resource depletion are but the latest foes to scar us. We will of course overcome because we are us, we are special; we need to survive until the sun burns out. We cannot become the cause of our own destruction, what a foolish end that would be. We must consider pride and ego our collective enemies as only pride and ego could push us towards human-made Armageddon.

I know we will continue surviving because that is what we do. It may seem to many that they are weak or fragile due to this modern capitalistic era where pampering and outsourcing and healthcare and life extension has become the new norm, but do not trick yourselves into believing that you are anything less than the most powerful being on the planet. Every human is the Apex, we represent the greatest achievement of evolution and strength and indomitability. We are each of us the legacy of unimaginably strong ancestors, ancestors who shielded their young from ice ages and sabre-toothed tigers; ancestors who conquered fear and fate again and again down throughout the ages, millennia before Jesus or Mohammad walked the earth.

Some people may believe that the one and only solution to creating peace in the Middle East is to make the entirety of the region Muslim. To such folk I respond:

What religion does Iran subscribe to? What religion does Iraq subscribe to? What religion does Qatar subscribe to or Saudi Arabia? All Islam, yet these nations have recently warred against one another—Muslim nations clashing with Muslim nations, Muslims killing Muslims. Islam does not guarantee peace.

How was it possible that the Iran/Iraq war lasted for so many years? How was it possible that 50 Scud missiles were, not all that long ago (First Gulf War), fired into Saudi Arabia from Iraq?

So many years when those sympathetic in the West to the concerns/plight/defeat of the Palestinians remained absolutely silent, why?

Because the folk who are in 2024 siding with Palestinians and Gaza only seem to become angered and enraged when Jews kill Muslims. This is why that terrible war between the neighbours Iran and Iraq was so bloody, so long and so protracted, because there wasn't a Jew in sight.

Removing Jews from the Middle East, their ancestral homeland where they have buried their dead for thousands of years, since a time long before the Islamic Ottoman Empire conquest of Israel/Palestine, is not the guarantor of peace as no two Muslim nation states anywhere on planet Earth wish to combine together and unite. All are separate and all wish to remain separate. Tell me, if every nation across the world vanished tomorrow except for Muslim nations, would tanks and guns and bullets and barbed wire no longer be constructed on our beautiful and miraculous spaceship that we call Earth?

Of course Muslim nations would continue manufacturing and stockpiling weapons and training their soldiers to kill the soldiers of other Muslim nations, even after Christianity and Judaism were removed from existence and the earth. No Muslim nations, not a single one desires for an international peaceful, demilitarised caliphate as tribalism and nationalism and pride and ego (and the individual interests of elites) dictate the course of every nation, which includes every Muslim nation.

Imagine every Jew and Christian left the Middle East, left their home.

Suddenly no one in that region could complain again about Jews or America; suddenly all would have to be responsible and self-supporting and set about building a future for themselves in a world without Jews and Christians. Before too long the Palestinians would encounter friction with their neighbours, with Lebanon and Egypt and other Arab Muslim nations who would see them as direct competitors, enemies even. The "allies" Palestinians believe they have are but temporary allies. For instance, leftists in the West are only allies due to the existence of Jews. Once the Jews have fled, Palestine will lose the left, they will lose them completely and immediately. What leftist voices tried to end the bloodshed between Muslim Iran and Muslim Iraq? Few to none.

More so, with Israel gone, why would Egypt or Lebanon or any of the Gulf states have any more interest in the Palestinian situation?

They would all likely be cautious in regards to trade and in regards to accepting in too many migrant workers from Palestine. The solution is not to remove Jews or to remove Christians as the endgame resulting from this would be a near repeat of what occurred between Iran and Iraq as none of the current well-established Arab Muslim nations desire for a strong and powerful Palestine to rise. Think about this. None of Palestine's "friends" desire for a strong and powerful and unified Palestine to develop and evolve as that would constitute a threat to them and necessitate a sharing of resources and land. If Jews and Christians were removed from their ancestral lands in the Middle East, would the Palestinians be laissez faire in regards to protecting and securing their borders? Of course not, and who would they be guarding their new borders from?

That's right, fellow Muslims. Instantly, absolutely instantly, Muslims in Gaza and other Palestinian territories would begin pointing their rifles and missiles at Muslim nations such as Lebanon and Egypt and the Gulf states whilst Palestinian diplomats and ambassadors lunched with their counterparts in the Arab League and engaged in trade negotiations. None of this would be a love-in or love fest; removing Jews would only quicken the descent into war in the region.

Let us not forget that Judaism has never tried to convert other nations, whereas the only reason Islam is present within the region in question is due to Islamic conquests in the past. If the precedent is 'you keep what you conquer' (as in the case of Muslim conquests and historic victories) why is it that anyone complains about Israel occupying territory once owned/occupied by others?

Why is it that only Islam and Arabs keep what they conquer? Is it not fair play to respect any nation, any tribe who has the strength and tenacity and hutzpah to enlarge their nation? Is this not how the Ottoman Empire came to be in Palestine? Is this not how the British Empire, who defeated the Ottoman Empire, came to be in Palestine? Is this not how the Jews came to be in possession of the majority of Palestine and so forth?

Removing Jews is not only unjust (they are a biblical people, they are not foreigners), it is also unwise. For so long as the Jews and Christians remain in Israel/Palestine the world will continue to be watching and will continue to care, but if they left, no one would care what happened next to the Palestinians, just as leftists in the West did not care one iota when Muslim Iraqis killed Muslim Iranians and vice versa.

***

If you ask most folk, 'How will we create peace in the Middle East?' they will look to the ground; they will shrug and say something like, 'Only God knows,' or, 'I wish I knew.'

Once such people have read this book, it will provide hope and inspiration to them and all others who desperately seek to avert the easily avertable, the complete destruction of the Middle East.

I had just completed the writing of the Ukrainian peace book (*How We Will Create Peace in Ukraine and the World*) when the current conflict in

Gaza/Israel erupted, which is why my mind was on peace and resolution rather than on anger and thoughts of tribalistically siding with either the Arab underdog or the powerful Jewish State, a nuclear nation armed with Apache helicopters and modern American aviation and all manner of tanks and advanced weaponry. This is why so many in the West have sided with Hamas/the Palestinians, yet also a great many anti-Semites have used the conflict as a means to engage in a bit of old-fashioned Jew bashing.

It is because I know it serves no practical use for foreigners to choose sides, something I refrained from doing throughout that expansive 180,000-word book relating to peace in Ukraine/Russia, that I am not taking a side in this conflict beyond saying, 'Deliberately killing civilians on either side is wrong.'

This book will be as impartial as the Ukrainian peace book. I do not have a dog in this fight, I don't wish to see another Israeli or another Arab die in this conflict as life will kill us all in the end, it is nonsensical to speed up this process. We have so much more in common than not, with doctors on both sides being killed, mechanics on both sides being killed, journalists on both sides being killed—humanity is killing humanity.

A lot of ego and pride will have to be swallowed by all parties in order for the following suggestions and ideas to be digested and considered, which I know would not be suitable during times of peace and prosperity; rather, everything suggested here, as disagreeable as these ideas initially may seem, are intended as a last-ditch attempt to prevent the Middle East imploding fully, which will drag all Arab nations into the conflict and thereafter the USA and Russia, which will set the scene for WWIII.

This is why I urge one and all to imagine we are one day away from nuclear annihilation when you read the following words. This is why I ask for pride and ego to take a back seat because sometimes in life we must do the thing we dread the most in order to ensure the greatest outcome for ourselves, our children and for humanity, even if that means adopting one of the following solutions for an eternal and lasting peace in the Middle East.

If my every idea is rejected, please volunteer a few of your own, whoever you are, wherever you hail from. Minds must come together. Use my ideas as a foundation for your ideas and plans and then others will improve upon your ideas and plans until finally agreement is made and peace, a real and lasting peace, is won.

Chapter Four — Two Important Questions and an Important Point

Does Saudi Arabia or Iran or Syria desire for Palestine to come to possess her own navy and stockpile of nuclear missiles?

Does anyone think there would suddenly be peace in the Middle East if every Jew, both boy and girl and man and woman, all collectively vacated Israel in 2025, all settling in Middle America somewhere?

No to the first and no to the second as the false and childish belief that 'with Jews gone there will be peace and paradise on Earth in Palestine/Israel/the Middle East' is disproven by the fact that no two Muslim nations, no two Arab nations get along all that well. Look at the destructive and terrible war between Iran and Iraq in the 1980s for instance (all Muslim, all killing one another 24/7) or at the Iraqi invasion of Kuwait as another example.

There is not one Muslim nation, there are fifty Muslim nations, and ironically the loose alliance sometimes seen in the Arab world is only in existence due to the state of Israel being in existence—Jews keep Muslim unity alive. No more Jews = the end of the love fest between otherwise competing and very nationalistic Middle East and African states.

Gone be the Jews, thus starts the REAL Middle East wars.

It is essential in this hour to create a long-term peace solution in order to ensure no more terrorism, no more kidnapping, no more terror tunnels, no more aid or NGOs being needed and no more innocent Gazan men, women or children being needlessly caught up in the battle between the stabilising and democratic state of Israel and militarised political factions who desire endless battles with an unbeatable foe—unbeatable because there are many places Palestinians can move to in the region, but Jews, Jews only have Israel as Iran will not take them in, nor will Syria, nor will any Muslim nations in fact.

Yet, without Jews and Judaism there would be no Christianity and without Judaism in tandem with Christianity there would be no Islam; these religions, these cultures, these peoples are interlinked and should all survive and thrive. In this nuclear age, when it seems your state is about to fall as you are surrounded by an attacking enemy baying for blood, of course you will reach out to push the nuclear button if you have one nearby, which Israel does, which France does, which many nations possess. Wouldn't

France push the button if the French people and French culture and the French state and territory were all in imminent threat? Of course they would, again and again and again.

And here is the important point that should be considered before reading any details about the plans that will follow or the additional supplementary chapters.

The point relates to democracy, transparency, honesty and justice.

I include here a section from another book, the book in which I end conspiracy theorism. I include this section here as it demonstrates how democratic, transparent and honest the state of Israel is in contrast to her nearest neighbours. Palestinians have been guarding the people who kidnapped, raped and killed young people partying at a music festival, whereas the Jewish people have consistently thrown their leaders into jail; the difference is night and day.

Corruption in Gaza and the Palestinian territories is, according to the Israelis, enabled to continue and a widespread practice and reality causing mass misery for the Palestinians, whereas in Israel, the corrupt, even if they are in high office and have many shekels in the bank and many powerful friends, find themselves dragged to court and frequently thereafter thrown into jail.

Surely all Palestinians want corruption and crime and abuses of power to end?

Surely they desire for a system similar to that which exists in Israel to replace the current order they find themselves living within, which currently means aid dependency, unelected officials, militancy and being dragged into conflicts with nuclear powers?

Question Eleven

(From the book The Truth at Last! 33 Essential Questions for Conspiracy Theorists*)*

Why does Israel publicly expose crimes and abuses of power carried out by her elected officials, even jailing both a former prime minister and a former president of Israel, if 'all Jews are the same' and are all 'on the same Zionist page'?

***

Firstly, to those who claim Israel is a dictatorship or the protector of Jews everywhere, even if they are criminals, the fact that Olmert was sentenced to six years in prison (he served most of that term) fully dispels that myth. Not only is Israel a democracy, it is one of few nations in the history of the world to have ever imprisoned a prime minster, kudos to Israel.

Israel knows that whenever she publicly announces crimes and misdemeanours committed by high-ranking Israeli officials her detractors from near and far may utilise this information for propaganda purposes; it would be far more prudent for a nation that hates democracy and all non-Jews to simply lie, right? This proves that Israel doesn't hate others as much as some conspiracy theorists have claimed because the conspiracy theories involving Jews and Israel, including the now massively debunked Protocols of Zion (which includes vast tracts that were clearly lifted/plagiarised from previously published works), all paint a picture of a very cunning, deceitful and cohesive Zionist people who all wish to save Barabbas…

Every time Israel imprisons a corrupt official, every time Israel arrests a former prime minister or president the Israelis are proving their impartiality, proving they care about the rule of law and proving that they are committed to honesty, transparency, democracy and openness. This is why anti-Semites don't crow about the good things Israel does such as imprison their own bad guys or shame their own leaders and elites, because this disproves the stereotypes and dispels the myths that all Jews are united, tribal and a danger to humanity, rather than just another tribe trying to survive in this crazy world of ours.

Former Jewish President of Israel Moshe Katsav was arrested and imprisoned for seven years for multiple crimes by Israel.

Former Jewish Prime Minister of Israel Ehud Olmert was arrested and imprisoned for six years for multiple crimes by Israel.

Former Jewish Minister Schlomo Benizri was arrested and imprisoned for 18 months for multiple crimes by Israel.

Former Jewish Minister Aryeh Deri was arrested and imprisoned for three years for multiple crimes by Israel.

Former Jewish Minister Gonen Segev was arrested and imprisoned for 11 years for multiple crimes by Israel.

Former Jewish Knesset member Ofer Hugi was arrested and imprisoned for two years for multiple crimes by Israel.

Former Jewish Mayor Zvi Bar was arrested and imprisoned for five and a half years for multiple crimes by Israel.

Former Ashkenazi Chief Rabbi Yona Metzger was arrested and imprisoned for three and a half years for multiple crimes by Israel.

The list above proves two things:

1/ That Jews are human like all of us, they are no different from anyone else, fallible and capable of making mistakes.

2/ That there is no global Jewish conspiracy to hurt, attack and dominate non-Jews because Israelites seem to spend most of their time smashing Jewish corruption, exposing Jewish crimes and ensuring that Israel becomes ever more democratic. How many corrupt officials in the West have ever seen the inside of a jail cell? Far too few, if any, is the answer.

Chapter Five — Extremism, "Terrorists" and Dresden

The term "terrorist" is overused and is the cause of much ire as it in effect dehumanises he who is called a terrorist.

In the eyes of the British, George Washington was a terrorist, as were those heroic peasants who stormed the Bastille.

Having said that, are Hamas and Hezbollah terrorists? Folk are divided on this issue, so how about another question instead?

Are Hamas and Hezbollah more extreme than the NDSAP and are Gazan and Palestinian civilians more radical and indoctrinated than the citizens of the Third Reich?

I ask this question because the Germans tolerated the French, the British, Americans and Russians occupying them, ridding their land of certain political parties and belief systems, whereas the Palestinian leadership and people resist both of these things, seemingly choosing death rather than compromise and peace.

The German people suffered terribly after the bombing of Dresden, a city housing civilians, the injured and non-combatants, which was firebombed, utterly wiped out by the Allies, resulting in Hiroshima-level loss of life; yet no one anywhere suggested the surviving women and children and remnants of the NSDAP found in the ashes of that felled city should be permitted self-rule and self-governance as a result of being so harmed by their foe. No, that would have been absurd, just as it is absurd to permit any defeated foe to be left alone to rebuild, to reinforce and to train up the next generation to continue the generational fight against neighbouring tribes.

If you hate Arabs, encourage more Hamas and Hezbollah resistance; if you hate Arabs and Palestinians and Gazans insist that more aid floods into the Middle East to help prop up the undemocratic organisations and "parties" that govern the long-suffering folk in places such as Gaza as aid to the Middle East and supporting groups many consider to be terrorists is what led to this bleak moment in history. Whereas, if the 'Allies come in', like they did in 1945, a new peaceful order and trust will be instantly created.

Will pride have to be swallowed? Yes, just as it was for tens of millions of Germans forced to live under occupation for fifty years in the heart of

Europe not so very long ago, but will those living under occupation be alive, at peace, healthy and eventually hopeful and happy? Yes, for a certainty, the answer is yes, but first we need to eradicate this sectarian hate. We need elections, we need a restoration of democracy—in Gaza the last election took place in 2006....

I do not want any nations to be destroyed in 2025, yet that is perhaps what will certainly occur in the Middle East unless radical, peaceful change takes place, with peace plans of course emanating from Arab and Muslim states being mistrusted and thus rejected by Israel and the USA and the same applies to Israeli and US plans being rejected by the collective Middle East. Yet the plans offered herein are neutral, nonpartisan and conceived solely out of a desire to end the bloodshed and hate, end the generational suffering and finally bring to an end the needless instability and discord in the Middle East, a land that should be full of scholars and peace and brotherhood, not AK47s, drones, kidnappings and racial hatred.

We can create peace in the Middle East. We must create peace in the Middle East. We *will* create peace in the Middle East.

Chapter Six — The Saudi Proposal
Option One

Not being Jewish, Arab, Muslim or a political radical one way or the other means that I am impartial in terms of proffering peace advice and suggestions to my Arab and Jewish cousins in the Middle East; however, I do have an opinion in regards to which of the five means to create peace I prefer.

It is the Saudi Proposal that I find myself drawn towards supporting most strongly of all. I say this not to be leading but to be honest, with this plan not necessitating conflicts, war, coups or bloodshed of any kind.

The Saudi Proposal for a myriad of complex reasons will create lasting peace in the Middle East. Yet I caution; with Middle Eastern states no longer able to attack Israel, which will be the end result of the Saudi Proposal, these states may very well return to fighting among themselves, as was the case back in the 1980s when Muslim Iran was locked in a death battle with her Muslim neighbour Iraq, with Israel at that time, most folk in 2024 will be shocked to learn, supporting Iran, an ally during that dangerous period of time that caused the untimely deaths of hundreds of thousands of Iranians and Iraqis, including many Iranian child-soldiers.

Yes, there is scope for Muslim nations and competing Shia and Sunni ideologies to clash in the Middle East once the Palestinian issue has been settled once and for all following the implementation of the Saudi Proposal, but we can address such issues as and when they arise. Today, the civilians of Palestine and Israel need to be protected and escalation needs to be avoided to prevent those same Muslim and Arab nations ceasing to be as a result of further miscalculations and the false belief that Israel 'doesn't have the teeth' to bite back. She has proved she has teeth as the complaints and threats emanating from the ICC in this hour fully attest.

Those who hate Israel will not be in love with the Saudi Proposal, yet those who love peace and optimism and who honestly wish to safeguard Gazan children will wholeheartedly adore this proposal and I suspect the Kingdom of Saudi Arabia, the seat of Islam, will similarly adore this means to end the bloodshed and sectarianism once and for all, with Saudi Arabia becoming peacemaker and Palestine saver.

***

Followers of international politics, especially goings on in the fractious Middle East, will know of Israel's deep desire to forge a good working relationship with the kingdom of Saudi Arabia.

This is a smart and pragmatic move, one which would, over time, cause all of the Muslim lands in the region to treat Israel and Israelis with more respect as they witnessed them breaking bread with a Muslim nation and engaging in no small amount of mutually beneficial trade and tourism also.

So let us imagine that relations do improve between these two nations, these two tribes, in the coming months, their cooperation and potential partnering having been harmed no end by the October 7th attack and the predictable Israeli backlash—try kidnapping my loved ones, try invading my land, I, you, he, her; all would react in the same manner.

Imagine Saudi Arabia and Israel were best friends as we enter 2025 as you consider the ramifications and workability of the Saudi Proposal, which will follow.

In order to ensure against repeats of October 7th, those who were behind that attack, most will agree, need to be removed from Palestine and preferably from the entire region. Perhaps a liberal nation such as Canada or Germany, which have been heavily critical of Israel's response to the mass murder, mass rape and mass kidnapping attack on October 7th, would like to import and house the ranks of Hamas and perhaps also the leadership of Hezbollah? If not, such states should refrain from unhelpful criticism and condemnation.

Of course long-term stability and safety is necessary in order for Israel to begin producing and importing fewer weapons, which is what I desire, to begin de-escalation, to increase aid and support to Gaza and to increase cooperation with Gaza and the Palestinian territories as a whole. So how do we achieve this?

We cannot use the UN due to their ranks, admittedly so, being heavily infiltrated by Hamas and Hamas-supporting radicals, with the UN recently sacking a dozen or so workers who were involved in the UNRWA and in terrorism and barbarism and inhumanity it also seems; such is the allegation coming out of Jerusalem these days.

The UN has taken sides for the longest time and their people and agencies are not trusted by Israel, so no UN solution is possible as when the UN were in Gaza and when NGOs were in Gaza, the terror tunnels expanded by the day right under their feet and democracy came crashing to a halt as new sociopathic radicals were birthed and multiplied and as Iran came to fund and control the actions of a minority in Gaza/Palestine/Lebanon all whilst the UN, aid agencies and NGOs continued attacking and critiquing Israel, creating a war for Israel on multiple fronts.

The UN is to be kept out of it, as are NGOs, as are all aid agencies—they have not enabled peace; rather, they have only enabled violent groups to rearm, to expand operations, to increase their stranglehold on power and to dominate an entire people into continuing to tolerate tunnels being constructed, continuing to tolerate all those thousands of rockets being constructed and continuing to tolerate living in an inglorious aid-dependent embarrassing reality whereby the "heroes and leaders" hide in holes in the ground whilst the people above are fed by compassionate foreigners.

The UN, aid agencies and NGOs have only made matters worse, consistently. Israel will never again tolerate their interference, mismanagement, bias, critique or enablement of terrorism.

But what about Saudi Arabia?

The international community would be loath to tolerate every inch of Palestinian land being occupied and settled by Israelis, it would of course be 'bad PR' for Israel to seize all of the disputed land in question, unlike in WWII when it was 'good PR' to seize and occupy Japan and Germany.

Perhaps if Hamas had succeeded in killing 500,000 Jews in October the international community and in particular the progressive liberal West would have deemed it proportional, necessary, vital even, for Israel to expand in all directions, even into Lebanon and Yemen and Iran if necessary, in order to get respect, in order to deter any other direct assault on the state of Israel and to, in the long-term, give all peoples in the Middle East a good quality of life—a life without tunnels and kidnapping and rocket attacks and unending fear and radicalism and children raised to hate Jews on a cellular level, no longer viewing them as human beings but as aliens, as things, as animals and as trophies to be won and owned, which are hurriedly spirited away into tunnels and hiding places by "heroic" freedom fighters.

So where does Saudi Arabia factor in? How could that wealthy and influential kingdom assist Israel and Palestine?

The Saudis would be trusted by other nations in the region, trusted by the Palestinian people owing to them being a fellow Muslim nation and trusted by Israel following closer ties and the forging of a cast-iron non-aggression pact.

US 'boots on the ground' in Israel and Palestine would be disastrous, just terrible PR, as would an injection of soldiers from any of the nations who previously possessed empires or colonies, with the protests in Western nations expected long before Brits or Germans or French or American soldiers boarded the first transport planes headed to Gaza, Lebanon and elsewhere if needed (in order to prevent WWIII) to long serve as peacekeepers as their grandfathers did in Germany not all that long ago.

To avoid the noisy protests and fake indignation and cries of 'fascist' and 'occupier' and other such nonsense, the solution could very well be Saudi Arabia.

Saudi troops.

Saudi oversight.

Saudi infrastructure.

Saudi know-how.

Saudi leadership—peaceful leadership.

And Saudi hutzpah and pragmatism.

If the peace between Israel and Saudi Arabia was predicated upon Saudi Arabia maintaining the peace in Palestine, Saudis smashing every terror plot, Saudis preventing the building of a single tunnel and Saudis ensuring that the citizens they oversee and protect by their presence are well fed, housed, nurtured, and educated, what a glorious long-term peace would lie ahead.

Over time, the people of Gaza would come to prefer living under a new authority, the Saudi Muslim authority, with every peacekeeper a Muslim, a peaceful Muslim from Saudi Arabia who is there to protect Palestine and the people of Palestine.

Before long, the folk of Gaza would reject militancy and armed resistance; they would melt down their AK47s, they would report every tunnel being dug to the Saudi Authorities. It would be akin to the Allied occupation of Germany post 1945, but rather than the "winning side" coming to be the occupiers, which would be a huge blow to Palestinian pride and morale, it would be neutral and impartial Saudis who were maintaining order, ensuring good long-term stability and guaranteeing, absolutely guaranteeing that never again could a rocket be launched in the direction of Israel from any neighboring territory as the message that would be sent out far and wide as a result of the Saudi proposal would be:

'Attack Israel and your terror leaders who desire violence and bloodshed and disorder and war shall be vanquished. Your infrastructure shall naturally be destroyed in our battle to protect ourselves and, afterwards, an ally such as Saudi Arabia shall come to occupy your territory who the peace-desiring citizens of your land will come to see as saviors and liberators as they cleanse your land of kidnappers and inciters.'

The ties that could come to bind Israel and Saudi Arabia together would grow infinitely stronger if the Saudi Proposal was enacted in the very near future as what would in effect be created would be 'new additions' to the territory of Saudi Arabia, with the Saudi flag coming to fly over Gaza and even over Lebanon and elsewhere if attacks continued to emanate from such territories.

A peaceful and wise Muslim nation who tolerates no terrorism, who tolerates no fractiousness or mobs or terror tunnels, would be intrinsically beneficial to the long-term survival of the state of Israel.

Imagine, suddenly, that Gaza became Saudi territory.

Immediately the ramifications of this move would be a nullifying of the belief that Israel wishes to settle Gaza or steal Muslim land as once the Saudi troops and infrastructure and Saudi aid and support and expertise arrived, bringing with them huge investment and willpower, Israel would never, could never, enter a demilitarized Palestine, with the Saudis ensuring on day one of their long-term peacekeeping and rebuilding mission that no violence would take place, no new tunnels would be built, rockets would be a thing of the past and that foreign players such as Iran would now have nothing to do with Israel, Lebanon or Palestine.

This move would benefit everyone in the long-term.

Peace between Saudi Arabia and Israel would be guaranteed, this precedent setting the scene for the Jewish state of Israel being accepted, respected and befriended throughout the remainder of the Muslim world. This would be the start of a peaceful new future, one which would involve the continuing existence of both Judaism and Islam.

The cold war between Iran and Israel could hurriedly end as Saudi Arabia would come to broker trade agreements between Israel and Iran, Israel's new best friend in the region opening doors, calming fears and enabling peace overtures continually as momentum would build and build in a single peaceful and optimistic direction as weapon production decreased everywhere, most importantly in Palestine and Iran and Yemen and Lebanon.

The people of Gaza would now have a neutral governor in the form of Saudi Arabia. There would be no more hate, no more angst, no more recriminations and certainly no more suicide vests as a result of every single Palestinian knowing full well that the Saudis were there to protect them, knowing full well that they understood their struggle and past; that they empathised and wished them well.

The Jewish people would immediately benefit also, knowing that the days of being bashed by the UN and the international press, NGOs and political radicals would be over because, henceforth, when terror tunnels were uncovered and attacked, when militants' homes were bulldozed and when militants and anti-democratic forces in Palestine who sought to nihilistically drag the region into a perpetual state of tribalist bloodshed were fought against and defeated, it would be Saudis doing the fighting and defeating rather than the sons and daughters of Israel. Conscription in Israel would be dialed back; fewer Israelis would be seen out and about with rifles casually slung over their shoulders, even on beaches and in parks and cafes, as is the case today tragically.

The only folk who would not prosper from the Saudi solution would be anti-Semites and those who have come to habitually scapegoat Jews and the state of Israel for everything, especially for their own failures, shortcomings, corruption and inept leadership and flawed stewardship.

When the Saudis had arrived, when it became obvious that they would not be leaving any time soon, as the move perhaps became a necessary permanent arrangement, why would there be any anger in Gaza directed towards Israel? The war would be over; that is what the arrival of ten thousand Saudi peacekeepers would herald. Peacekeepers supported by hundreds of Saudi companies and workers who would in a small space of time rebuild that which was destroyed in the pursuit of rescuing the stolen sons and daughters of Israel.

With the war ended and Palestine's borders eternally safeguarded by the state of Saudi Arabia, there could no longer be hate or paranoia, there could no longer be AK47s or truck attacks or stabbing attacks or any other kind of attacks as every Palestinian would enter education or work, with none, not a single one being permitted by the Saudi authorities to engage in proscribed terrorist activities.

What would be the complaints about this proposal?

'Palestinians have a right to self-rule.'

'We don't trust Saudi Arabia.'

'Palestinians deserve to be free.'

Let us look at the undisputed evidence. The last election held in Gaza took place in 2006. Israel would welcome more elections and more democracy. Israel is not the cause of democracy being suspended in Gaza/Palestine.

It seems that when granted full autonomy and the ability to decide their own fate, the people of Gaza/Palestine desire to be represented by the likes of Hamas and continue to be represented by Hamas and are happy for democracy to, in effect, come to a quick and sudden end, so it is not as though the "freedom" that many foreigners believe the Palestinians desire centers around democratic norms or a desire to be free but, rather, this "freedom" is in fact a reference to the right of Palestinians to be steered by an authoritarian one-party state—which, troublingly, desires the state of Israel to cease to exist.

Irrespective of complaints about this proposal, it may be deemed a necessary move and one we may come to witness before 2030 as a preference to nuclear escalation.

You could not have permitted the remnants of the NSDAP to rebuild Germany after WWII, that would have been absurd; neither could you have refrained from occupying that vast nation owing to Germany launching unprovoked attacks on her neighbours.

The October 7th provocation benefited Iran and her partners primarily as it would of course push Israel and Saudi Arabia apart, leading to Saudi Arabia criticizing Israeli actions following that brutal assault and more recently even engaging in naval exercises alongside Iran. Those gruesome attacks last October, which led to the unpleasantness we have borne witness to in Gaza, massively aided Iran, disrupted relations and trade talks and cooperation between Israel and Saudi Arabia and many astute observers will be of the opinion that that was the real motivation for the attacks, that harming the natural and logical alliance between Jerusalem and Riyadh was the goal all along.

Put yourself in the shoes of one of the invaders who kidnapped and killed all of those Israeli children on October 7th; would you think, for even a second, that Israel would not respond?

Would you imagine hiding away in tunnels under hospitals and schools would deter Israel from seeking justice?

If the answer is yes, if the leadership of Gaza/Palestine truly believed their actions would 'cow Israel' this would serve to prove why a new authority, perhaps a Saudi authority, and a peace-ensuring mission is fundamentally necessary as soon as possible as any reasonably minded fellow would know that October 7th would of course result in huge loss of life on both sides, billions in damages, infrastructure being smashed and any dream of having an independent, respected and sovereign state going up in smoke.

It seems clear that Gaza was sacrificed, that the folk who engaged in these attacks were mere pawns, mere proxies, whose real mission was to prevent Saudi Arabia and Israel becoming friends, that the true intention of the brazen assaults and kidnappings and murders on October 7th was to prevent the peaceful union of Jerusalem and Mecca, of Israel and Saudi Arabia—which is why, perhaps, just perhaps, Israel and Saudi Arabia should now fight tooth and nail to become closer than ever before, and surely the Saudis, desiring long-term peace and stability in the region and desiring to lead, rather than merely watch on from the sidelines, would warmly welcome the chance to rebuild Gaza, to end all terrorism in the region, to achieve great acclaim for her people and state by raising her flag over Palestine and in so doing ushering in the longest period of peace and prosperity ever witnessed in the Middle East.

Together, Israel and Saudi Arabia would be a force for peace and good; together they would ensure the Palestinian people were protected from terrorist threats from within and from the financiers of terrorism from abroad as, from day one of the Saudi peace-keeping mission, not a single penny or cent would be allowed to enter Gaza or Palestine unless that money was headed towards children, the needy, the disabled and the non-combatants. A robust, unwavering and uplifting intervention and occupation by Saudi Arabia would change everything.

Despite this course of action seeming unexpected, bizarre even, if everything else attempted so far has failed, if diplomacy and clashes and imprisonment and incursions and IDF operations of every type have all come to nothing, and if the UN and their aid agencies can neither be trusted nor are the long-term solve needed to starve terror groups and defund the sociopaths dragging the Middle East towards endless pointless violence and conflict, of course the Saudi Proposal deserves airtime, consideration and debate because, even if this is no one's first preference, it is a workable solution.

It will end hate and terrorism, it will end the voices in the West screaming anti-Israel rhetoric 24/7, and, most importantly, it will reassure every living Gazan and Palestinian that they never again need to fear Israel or the IDF or Mossad because they are now protected by Saudi Arabia, the nation of Mecca and Medina. They are now protected by the seat of Islam. Gone will be the anger, gone will be the violent mobs, and gone will be the sectarianism, replaced with beautiful hope, optimism, growth, enthusiasm, love and precious and joyous peace.

Without peace, we are animals; with peace we are human.

Can you have 'road rage' with a neighbor whom you recognize on the road? No. You can only road rage against a stranger, who you do not know, who you believe is from far away, which is why once Saudi Arabia is Israel's next-door neighbor, with her administrators and troops located in Gaza/Palestine, Israel can never road rage against Saudi Arabia and Saudi Arabia can never get involved in road rage with Israel.

When far apart, the chances of a battle massively increase; whereas, when suddenly neighbors, the two powerful states would be forced to become the very best of friends, with this reality never changing, which would ensure eternal peace in the Middle East.

Chapter Seven — The Donbas 'No Man's Land' Peace Plan

Option Two

This Plan, which is referred to as 'Plan B' in the book *How We Will Create Peace in Ukraine and the World*, will assuredly reduce tensions immediately if implemented yet would require some careful tweaks from the original plan, which is offered to the Russian and Ukrainian peoples as a means to bring about a lasting peace and as a means to avoid future disputes down the line.

The Donbas plan, in brief (the entire plan will be reproduced below), seeks to end the conflict by declaring the contested landmass 'no man's land', as in, the international community recognises neither side's claim to the land.

The Donbas, in Eastern Ukraine or in Western Russia, depending upon your viewpoint and partisan side, being fully vacated as though contaminated with nuclear radiation and unliveable, would calm tensions in Ukraine and in Russia, would dissuade other nations from engaging in physical confrontations and border disputes with one another (fearing their conflict would end similarly, in mutual loss of territory) and would ensure that neither side felt their pride being wounded long after the end of the conflict. When a thief steals your apple, you are angered; yet, if he drops the apple, if it becomes lost to him, you can tolerate the loss of that which you desired to keep for yourself, this resolution perhaps not delighting you, but much of the emotional hurt will be gone once you know that no one benefited as a result of the action of the other, equality and harmony being created.

Of course Donbas is more than an apple and of course so is Gaza, which is why compensation would be necessary in both instances, with that necessity being addressed within the Ukrainian peace book.

In terms of Gaza, if the no man's land plan were to be implemented, it would look something like this:

A large swathe of territory on both sides of the border between Israel and Gaza being declared, eternally so, a demilitarised no man's land, with both sides ceding land, not to another party or state but sacrificing land and resources. That sacrifice, that loss of many square miles of good earth and minerals and territory, would be the precedent and lesson that would serve to prevent future flare-ups and clashes and disputes between these two very long-term neighbours.

In contrast, however, to the Ukrainian version of the Donbas no man's land plan, which, if enacted, would remove all soldiers, both Russian and Ukrainian, from the disputed areas immediately as those areas (in the contested region) would come to be considered 'new Chernobyls', uninhabitable areas forevermore, with the conflict being brought to a crashing halt upon the occasion of Russia and Ukraine agreeing like brothers, like good neighbours, to both agree never to set foot in the Donbas again, the Palestinian/Gazan iteration of no man's land, due to the long history of militant activities in the region, the construction of underground tunnels, and the fear that radicals will regroup and remilitarise, Israel would continue surveillance and counterterror activities both above and below ground, at least until such a time as free and fair elections were possible.

In the Israeli/Palestinian version of the Donbas plan, all of Gaza cannot be evacuated of humanity due to the very limited territory available to Palestinians. It is the abundance of land in both Russia and Ukraine that makes the possibility of Plan B working there viable and actionable in full with the complete evacuation of the Donbas possible in the shortest space of time, with that peace overture and means to end all future wars funded gladly by the international community as demonstrated within the Ukrainian peace book, it costing Western taxpayers very little to achieve that goal, in contrast to the costs of continuing to battle Russia and other adversaries in an endless and fractious cold war.

Both landmasses given up by both sides would be mined by each side as, yes, trust would be there, yet not blind trust, however, unlike the toxic situation on the North/South Korean border, the DMZ. There should not be a single soldier, nor a watch tower, nor a huge amount of military hardware as the gesture of enacting the no man's land solution is the final attempt at resolving disputes peacefully, meaning any incursion, any attempted invasion or reoccupation of the no man's land ceded by either side would be the prelude to total war, and, of course, both sides would be well aware of this.

In Total War, there are no longer civilians, there are no longer rules, which is why peace will be maintained as the alternative will be the mobilisation of every living Israeli and use of every weapon in their arsenal in order to once and for all ensure Jews can live in peace in the one and only nation they possess, unlike their adversaries who possess over fifty nations—fourteen million Jews and one Jewish nation in contrast to two billion Muslims and fifty Muslim nations.

In the Jewish/Palestinian iteration of Donbas, in addition to the no man's land naturally being mined, both states may also seek to embed subterraneous mines. The fear in Israel is that, at any moment, folk armed to the teeth will pop up out of the ground after accessing Israel via the use of underground tunnel networks; perhaps there is a similar fear in Gaza also.

We can nullify such fears by the use of subterranean mines and subterranean sensors, which will communicate to both sides whether or not the other is tunnelling or planning the launch of another October 7th type of attack.

Would a man wish to dig a tunnel if he thought he might strike an explosive mine with his pickaxe? Unlikely. We need to demotivate revenge, demotivate hate, and demotivate war and petty clashes, which only cause entire Palestinian towns and cities to be destroyed as Israelis seek to attack those who attacked them and stole away their daughters.

A joint sacrifice, both states surrendering land, would bring both sides together, would increase empathy and respect, and could, in the long-term, become the basis for peace and cooperation.

***

Plan B—A Dignified and Elegant Exit for Ukraine and Russia

(Chapter Ninety-One from the book *How We Will Create Peace in Ukraine and the World*)

'Our first task is ceasefire in the Donbas. I have been often asked: What price are you ready to pay for the ceasefire? It's a strange question. What price are you ready to pay for the lives of you loved ones? I can assure you that I'm ready to pay any price to stop the deaths of our heroes.'
— Volodymyr Zelenskyy, 20 May 2019.

In Summary:
- Russia does not win.
- Ukraine does not win.
- Peace wins.
- War ends, a draw is declared.
- The contested territory is demilitarised and peacefully depopulated completely.

Plan B (The 'No Man's Land' Peace Plan) restores lost pride and dignity, renews hope and relieves the unfathomable weight that currently rests upon the shoulders of Russians and Ukrainians—and once there is peace, once calm and order return, let no man raise his voice or allow himself to become angered, lest we lose what has been achieved, an impossible peace, a miracle for both nations and for the world.

The Donbas and Crimea are immediately demilitarised.

Russian armed forces leave Ukraine and territory occupied post 2014.

Plan B removes the Russian military presence from the Ukrainian mainland in seven days, creating a complete end to hostilities and demilitarisation within only one week.

The Donbas and Crimea (or more likely just the Donbas depending on negotiations, there is flexibility, there must be flexibility) become uninhabited, becoming an instant UNESCO World Heritage site—'No Man's Land' (an expansive forest, creating an uninhabited buffer between Russia and Ukraine), an eternal reminder of the pointlessness of war, an example of why we should always choose to talk, then listen, keep talking, listen some more and then talk some more until we have solved our problems, otherwise both sides will lose. We need to teach our children that victory cannot be achieved via war, that war itself is defeat.

Crimea, in this scenario, would be demilitarised immediately, whilst the Donbas would be concurrently demilitarised and depopulated also, with the majority of inhabitants being relocated to Russia, yet relocations to multiple locations would be possible if doing so would guarantee an incredibly swift end to this long and painful conflict.

Following demilitarisation, Crimea would again hold elections in regards to re-joining with Ukraine, remaining with Russia or becoming an independent state. However, in the eventuality of Plan B there would be no more elections or referendums in the east of Ukraine/west of Russia in the areas that are contested, which have changed hands numerous times over the years; rather, humanity would be removed from the soil completely—a huge peaceful and non-policed demilitarised zone and No Man's Land will have been created.

This huge gesture by both sides will be more than enough to deter future aggression and friction between the nations and tribes owing to all fearing their war and aggression and disagreements culminating in new 'No Man's Land' solutions—no nation would again be so willing to invade and no nation or union of nations would be so willing to provoke conflict and invasion.

Full-scale nuclear war is worse than all territory contested by Russian and Ukraine being eternally declared 'No Man's Land', as in, no man can ever have it, no man can place his flag there for the rest of time, no man can set foot in that (already) destroyed and tragic place. There's no need to remove the landmines, no need to rebuild; the entire territory will become a monument, it will be marked on all maps as 'No Man's Land', a reminder to others including the yet-to-be-born in China, Taiwan, the USA, India, Egypt, Turkey, Spain, Canada and every other nation that henceforth no nation can "win" wars and expand territory, that this precedent is fated to become the new status quo, repeated whenever leaders choose to abandon diplomacy and peaceful agreements and accords.

During the negotiation stage, the third parties who have kept the conflict alive via financing will be called upon to make concrete commitments to extend that same financing to ensure the peace is achieved via funding free houses/apartments for every Russian and Ukrainian man, woman and child living in the Donbas and future 'no man's land' territories the moment they agree to relocate to Russia or Ukraine or the EU/USA/rest of the world.

Those who financed war shall be called upon by all to finance the peace. The alternative will be more financing of war being required. Logic and common sense will prevail as Western leaders bankroll the reparations and compensation for many folk, massively softening the blow of moving house a few kilometres in one direction or the other.

Why would Ukrainians want to continue living in Communist-built concrete Soviet cities? Why would Ukrainians wish to rebuild these felled cities—monuments to Stalin?

The cost of this project will be covered by EU and NATO taxpayers, whose tax money is currently being used to produce billions of bullets and shells and weapons of every type. These taxpayers will be positively elated when told the fruits of their labours (their taxes) will now be repurposed and used only for humanitarian and peace-creating initiatives, such as the No Man's Land Peace Plan and the resettlement of the long-suffering residents of the affected areas, whom the world wants to protect and rehabilitate and give safe haven and nurture to.

Don't die for the Donbas; instead, choose to live for humanity. Every man who loves <u>Plan B</u> and desires to create the great forest loves humanity and peace.

The sacrifice made by those who voluntarily vacate once hostilities end will never be forgotten by a grateful world, with every soul who vacates achieving instant immortality for them and their family as the great forest will be the beginning of world peace, the beginning of the end of war. What a beautiful legacy for the great people of the Donbas.

***

Neither side (Russia/Ukraine) will be overjoyed; yet, at the same time, neither side would prefer WWIII as a preference to living in a world where this new non-inhabited landmass, 'No Man's Land', is a reality.

What wouldn't a man do to save his family, his nation and his planet?

Wouldn't a Russian sacrifice disputed land to save these things?

Wouldn't a Ukrainian sacrifice disputed land to save these things?

We can all win or we can all lose.

Objection Handling:

'But many people will have to be resettled.'—WWIII is worse.

'But we will lose many natural resources.'—WWIII is worse.

'But we don't want our country to lose any territory.'—WWIII is worse.

'We don't want anyone to tell us what to do.'—WWIII is worse.

The objections from both sides will be near identical.

***

Additional factors that lessen the blow of the joint abdication of sovereignty of the land in question by Ukraine and by Russia:

— Millions of Ukrainians will never voluntarily choose to return to Ukraine, the only thing in doubt is whether it will be three million or ten million souls who choose to make new lives elsewhere. If all of these many millions of people desired to return to Ukraine, it would be harder to implement the NML (No Man's Land) peace solution due to there being a need to rehouse these one-time Ukrainian citizens. However, as it stands (according to the diaspora in question, surveys, polls, interviews) most have no intention of returning even after peace has been secured.

— Ukrainian birth rates are dropping and they will continue to drop due to numerous factors. There is caution throughout Ukraine, there is rationing, this will last for some years, years where we will not see a surge in the Ukrainian population; the opposite will occur, it will continue to decrease until a decade has passed, once Ukraine is again strong and confident.

***

Due to the size of the land that would become NML (No Man's Land), a forest should be planted. Before long, nature will fully reclaim the land that man had a dispute over, which man sullied with war and violence and sectarianism and sadism.

The forest can be rapidly constructed using fleets of drones, which can sow seeds (rather than drop bombs) remotely, drones delivering seeds to build No Man's Land's forests (to produce oxygen, the new lungs of the East) using new technologies created on the fly such as weighted biodegradable 'seed bombs', which (when dropped from a height) will be able to penetrate even the hardest of soils in order to build the mightiest of trees (which will act as screening between the fraternal neighbours). I suggest drones for this purpose because so much of the territory in question is mined.

Both sides have installed untold thousands of mines there. This area will never be safe for human habitation and it certainly is not safe to physically plant trees, which is why technology could be leveraged to assist in the forestry proposal.

The money saved by not laboriously removing these untold thousands of land mines and the money saved by not rebuilding the infrastructure within this territory will aid New Ukraine in her quest to become independent in all ways as soon as physically and technically possible—and it is of course assumed that the entire world community will increase their financial donations to Ukraine if she bravely chooses this new direction until such a time as she no longer needs foreign help.

Repurposed drones: Drop seeds, not bombs.

***

The No Man's Land solution, the Donbas Peace Plan, <u>Plan B,</u> is a win-win rather than a lose-lose.

Unimaginable compensation would be provided for the peace-loving folk who choose to vacate this land in order to save the world. Peace, healing, reconciliation and moving forward with heads held high.

If this path is necessary it will certainly create waves of peace, which will wash over the entire earth, and I would call upon the world in the darkest hour as the war escalates beyond control, in those precious seconds we have left, as it seems impossible to pull back from the brink of total annihilation, from suicide, that as you reach out to turn that key you remember at least the No Man's Land solution, that you remember at least the Donbas Peace Plan, remember <u>Plan B</u>, that, rather than destroy civilisation and billions of lives, might we evacuate all soldiers and civilians from the disputed territories and thus avoid the Götterdämmerung?

***

In 100 years' time, a small Ukrainian boy might ask his father, 'Who lives there, Father, who lives in the great forest?'

To which his father will reply, 'No man lives there, Son, because that is No Man's Land. It belongs to no man because cousin killed cousin to possess that land and the War of the Cousins almost destroyed the world. This forest is an eternal reminder of the futility of war and inter-human violence, so tell your sons and daughters and your grandsons and granddaughters to avoid this forest. Entering it is forbidden because entering the forest will cause history to repeat itself; entering the forest will doom Ukraine and the world.'

Chapter Eight — The Iranian Resettlement Plan

Option Three

Would Israel, the USA and the EU be happy to fund the building of houses and apartment blocks for millions of people who chose to happily relocate to peaceful and stable Iran as a preference to continuing to live in a de facto warzone? Yes, and the cost would in fact be considerably less than is currently being spent on security, on aid, and on the production of expensive and divisive military hardware.

The only thing the Iranian side would provide would be the land, of which that nation has a great deal—each evacuee could live in a house, if they so chose, rather than being fated to live in an apartment as is the case in overpopulated urban areas such as Gaza City.

The Palestinian refugee camps, which exist in Jordan, Lebanon and Syrian as well as elsewhere including in the West Bank, are short-term fixes.

This peace plan is a hard sell to the Middle East because the issue of Palestinian sovereignty/claim to the aspects of the land acquired by the state of Israel via conquest (just as Arabs only came to be in Israel as a result of conquest, just as the British only came to own Palestine for a time as a result of conquest) is something Middle Eastern nations have long cited at the UN and when engaged in international diplomacy. It is the cause of multiple states receiving great Western sympathy and support over the years. As a result, this plan is indeed a hard sell as suddenly the Jewish scapegoat would be gone.

The Iranian resettlement plan would consist of the entire population of Gaza and other Palestinian enclaves relocating en masse to Iran. This may be thought by some as being the largest relocation of people in history, yet it is far from it. Many more Germans were relocated following WWII from many areas of Eastern Europe, many of whom (many of that huge number of millions of persons) had resided in those lands for generations, as Palestinians have in Palestine/Israel.

The Palestinian people would be safe in Iran, far from Israel, far from that former conflict, and would receive huge compensation for the stress and upheaval of relocating. They would all be considered altruistic heroes for volunteering to relocate in the interests of guaranteeing the Middle East does not 'go pop' once and for all—no one sane desires to see mushroom clouds rising over the Middle East. No one desires this.

A monumental relocation effort aided by the international community would take place with bricks and mortar being moved, entire buildings being moved if necessary in order to ensure a peaceful and amicable relocation and a lasting peace.

But what of the land that was vacated?

This land could not be settled by Israel in the eventuality of the Iranian resettlement plan as this would be seen as a victory for Israel and a step towards future expansionism and colonisation and domination—former Ottoman lands would fear that Israel was choosing to replicate the actions of the colonising Ottomans.

To avoid more fear and paranoia and to ensure the move was peaceful and that the Palestinian people living in New Palestine just outside of Tehran could make peace with the past, Gaza as well as the other territories in question now all vacated could be almost overnight transformed into 'Solar Cities', landmasses dominated by solar panels, reaching as far as the eye could see, constructed and installed and operated by Saudi Arabia, a neutral and trusted partner in the region, who would ensure that the electricity produced would illuminate every home in the new Palestinian towns and villages springing up in Iran, Palestine is a people, not a place.

Israel would not take this land, no; it would be similar to 'no man's land' with this act causing Israel's neighbours to respect and trust her more whilst serving to create greater bonds and friendships between neighbours such as Israel and Saudi Arabia, between Mecca and Jerusalem.

***

The Flight and Expulsion of the Germans

"Expulsion is the method which, insofar as we have been able to see, will be the most satisfactory and lasting. There will be no mixture of populations to cause endless trouble…. A clean sweep will be made. I am not alarmed by the prospect of disentanglement of populations, not even of these large transferences [he references the transference of 14.6 million Germans here], which are more possible in modern conditions than they have ever been before."
—Winston Churchill, the House of Commons, Dec 15th, 1944.

The participants at the Potsdam Conference asserted that expulsions were the only way to prevent ethnic violence.

Churchill was not pro-multiculturalism, as is evidenced by the above quote as well as his famous speech that spoke about fighting the invader wherever he dwelt, be it on beaches or landing grounds or anywhere else in between. This is the island spirit, this is Britain.

In his speech in the Commons, he was referencing a little known incident in history known as the 'Flight and Expulsion of the Germans', something that was deemed by him, the USA, Russia and many other nations an absolute necessity in order to prevent a third world war, in order to prevent the defeated Germans from being persecuted or massacred, and to ensure homogenous and separate and nationalistic nation states were created throughout Eastern and Western Europe—this was exceptional statecraft and statesmanship and courage.

The German people had spread out of what later became Germany over a period of several hundred years, spreading into Poland and Hungary and Romania as well as many other sovereign nations. Most were farmers and tradesmen who lived in a multicultural fashion, maintaining their identity and traditions and names and religion and customs, which spread mistrust and xenophobia, with many, including the Polish and Czechoslovakian Governments, imploring Churchill in as early as 1942 to remove the Germans from their territories after the fighting had been concluded (post WWII) in the interests of creating long-term peace, harmony and homogeny.

The extreme irony is only seventy years after Churchill warned about race riots and racial clashes and culture clashes resulting from continued multiculturalism in mainland Europe as a result of German migration, his monument in Central London required the protection of the Metropolitan Police due to it coming under attack by Black Lives Matter protesters, made possible solely due to the Crown and successive governments failing to heed his warning by undemocratically enforcing mass immigration and universally disliked and unworkable multiculturalism upon the UK and native peoples.

I agree with Churchill, just as I agree with the builders of the Great Wall of China, just as I agree with the builders of the huge walls of the Vatican— culture clashes are dangerous, racial clashes are dangerous and will always lead to either ethnic cleansing via expulsion (native flight) or war. There is no third possibility. It is 'fight or flight'.

The massive expulsion of the Germans from dozens of nations, which lasted almost a decade, has ensured a lasting peace in Europe, with 14.6 million people being relocated.

History evidences that 'resetting the board' works, which is why we should not discount out of hand the Iranian Resettlement Plan.

Chapter Nine — The United States of Israel

Option Four

The United States of Israel would come about after a devastating regional war, following Israeli-backed coups and assassinations, after lending her support to separatists and fifth columnists in competitor nations in the region which seek to 'wipe her off the map' and after NGOs, the UN and the Palestinian side and her supporters/backers all chose to reject the peace plans offered by Israel and impartial third parties and after the amicable and fair solutions provided in books such as this were rejected in full.

If Israel knows for a certainty that there will be constant, endless attacks directed at her; if Israel knows that her competitors are eternally committed to destroying her, wiping her off the Middle Eastern map, of course, in utter desperation, she will massively expand outwardly, very soon, as a result bringing about the creation of the United States of Israel, with Jerusalem and Israel the capital of a regional union of nations, all of which were "liberated" by her during a final battle for peace and stability. Only a foolish state would happily consent to being attacked forever, bullied and bitten and needled and belittled and disrespected forever, and Israel is no fool; nor are her people.

I suggest the USOI solution as well as Plan C should not come to be, until everything else has first been attempted, before all other avenues have been exhausted as a means to ensure the survival of Israel and her unique people and culture and her democracy. Her greatest ally, the USA, will provide arms, intelligence and latterly no doubt 'boots on the ground' if and when Israel feels the only option left to ensure self-defence in the long-term is to create the United States of Israel.

In addition to the USA, it is predictable that other Western partners would feel compelled to come to Israel's aid as she is attacked on all sides concurrently, with the absence of partners, with the absence of international support causing Israel to be backed into a corner, which would almost certainly cause her to lash out in a nuclear fashion.

To prevent nuclear war, European nations, the USA, Commonwealth nations, the UK as well as regional partners would join Israel in 'absorbing' Lebanon, Syria, Iran and potentially nations such as Yemen and Jordan also, all at once ending the rebellions and friction and rocket fire and kidnappings and unending fear and anxiety that plague the Middle East as well as the rest of the world.

To better understand the concept and the drive and the argument to create a unified group of nations in the Middle East under the democratic banner of Israel, supported to the hilt by her ally the USA and supported also by every nation desiring to stave off WWIII and a nuclear winter, I include a fictional speech that could be delivered by an Israeli Prime Minister upon the occasion of every peace overture and plan being resoundingly rejected by Palestinians, Hamas, Hezbollah, NGOs and the UN:

'To the people of Yemen, of Lebanon, of Iran, and of every other nation that directly or indirectly attacks Israel, we have a message for you, listen to it very carefully:

'If you are captive and if attacks continue to be launched from your lands against our precious and beloved people who refuse to live in fear, who will soon never need to enter an air raid shelter again; if you cannot control the groups and factions operating in your lands and controlling your fates and if you do not desire these groups and rebels and terrorists and similar proxies to remain in your lands, Israel will come to your aid. Israel will liberate your land and ensure that never again will terrorists operate in your land. Never again will you become caught in the crossfire; never again, I swear, will you need to fear war, because if attacks continue to be launched at Israel from your land, if the governments and armies of your land do not or cannot control your borders and the militants operating at will within your borders, if they have lost control of everything and fear the nations who back the terrorists and attackers of Israel, we will have no choice, Israel will have no choice but to step in, to create order and stability and peace and the restoration of civility in neighbouring lands and territories.

'If the cowardly attacks continue, if our people continue being attacked whilst your people remain hostages in your own lands as the enemies of peace and civilisation continue to surround you, endanger you, endanger Israel and the world, there will be an unprecedented response, and afterwards order and peace shall be restored as all peoples in the lands where the attackers and terrorists enjoy freedom and hospitality today shall be liberated fully tomorrow.'

The Israeli prime minster, if questioned about what he meant when he used the term 'liberated' would likely reply:

'Those lands have already been invaded by terrorist groups and bullies and killers. The people of these lands do not desire their presence a moment longer. Liberated means liberated.'

****

If folk continue ganging up on Israel and pushing her into a corner, of course it is natural and predictable for the rise of the United States of Israel to take place long before 2030 as a preference to nuclear war and as a preference to the complete destruction of the State of Israel, resulting in yet another Jewish exodus.

In this endgame, Muslim nations would come into a union with a Jewish nation. In this endgame, there would be no more rocket attacks, no more fighting, just as the horrendous fighting between Americans halted once the north and south joined together in union following their Civil War. If Lebanon became a member of the United States of Israel (working name, you understand, this would likely be finessed and tweaked), Israel would come to be the chief protector of the Lebanese people in the way that Washington in 2024 would destroy any foreign army who dared set foot in Texas!

Israel would become defenders of all the lands liberated in the war of survival, with it being assumed that proscribed groups often referred to as terrorists would be exiled, being relocated to sympathetic nations such as liberal Canada.

Would this solution please all? No, yet all would still be alive.

Is this solution what Israel wants or the majority of Israelis desire? No, absolutely not; yet, if the other peace proposals are rejected, what option will be left?

Israelis cannot abandon Israel; it is the one and only Jewish state. There can be no surrender, and with a union of states in the Middle East, a real union, cohesive and peaceful, true, progressive peace throughout the region, as well as in Africa and Asia, will be possible as an inspirational union of Jews and Muslims would lead the way in demonstrating that eternal war is not the solution; rather, peaceful unity is.

Chapter Ten — Plan C

Option Five

If everything else attempted fails, something known as Plan C, which comes to life in the book of the same name, *Plan C: Mutually Assured Survival*, may come to be required.

Plan C would certainly aid international peace and would also, importantly, prevent regional or international escalation of localised conflicts and disagreements. However, first I would strongly suggest the Saudi Proposal be considered, the Donbas No Man's Land Plan or the Iranian Resettlement as those peace overtures could negate the need for Plan C completely; yet for those who reject the Saudi Proposal, the resettlement plan, the Donbas peace plan and who do not wish to see the rise of the United States of Israel, I invite them to read Plan C.

If everything else fails, the strong, the wise and the forward thinking will implement Plan C, even if that is not what the majority desire, as an alternative to unending wars and political and social extremism spilling out of the Middle East and out of Western college campuses and threatening to disrupt good order and peace everywhere as the discontent and pain and suffering in Israel and Palestine become global and the fires ignited in the Middle East become the beginning of the end of civilisation as we know it.

Plan C is a part of the Peace Series of books for a good reason as it exists as a final fail-safe to ensure against cataclysms and the destruction of every state in the Middle East and beyond.

Chapter Eleven — The 51st and 52nd States of America

(Originally chapter Twenty-Nine from the book, *How We Will Create Peace in Ukraine and the World*, published December 10, 2023, written early January 2023, nine months prior to the October 7th attacks)

Russia is occupying (internationally recognised) Ukrainian territory as of 02/01/2023.

Israel is occupying (internationally recognised) Palestinian territory as of 02/01/2023.

Both Russia and Israel claim to be occupying these territories in order to ensure the protection of their nations.

Russia complains that the (USA based) UN is anti-Russia; Israel claims the same thing.

I had long wondered what Ukraine's position would be in 2023 in regards to the continuing occupation by Israel of the West Bank on the Jordan River, the claimed Palestinian territories. The Southern states of North America were once free and sovereign, until they were invaded and occupied by the stronger northern states. You only own what you can control and defend, which is why every child born in the Southern states is forced to swear allegiance every morning at school to the flag of the north, which is now their flag because their territory now belongs to everyone within the union their fathers were forced to join at gunpoint.

In previous years, Ukraine has agreed with the majority of the world community that the 'illegal' occupation of historic Palestinian lands should come to an end. On multiple occasions, Ukraine has voted against Israel and against the USA in this regard, resisting their collective will and political pressure, but this is now changing.

Ukraine cannot possibly only hate one occupier; she must hate all occupiers and colonisers or risk being accused of hypocrisy or even complicity. 'Ukraine needs to eject the occupiers … but Palestinians need to sit on their hands and be quiet.' If Ukraine makes this statement, the world will think twice before sending more weapons and aid to Kiev; many will be surprised to learn that this more or less already occurred.

The 'big change' in terms of the official Ukrainian state policy towards the issue of occupation in Palestine occurred just two days ago, on December 30th, 2022, when Ukraine had an opportunity (via the UN) to help fellow victims of occupation but chose not to. The shared experience of being occupied was not enough for Ukraine to continue her support of the Palestinians.

The UN Committee on Special Political and Decolonization Affairs' attempt to resolve the issue of the occupation of the West Bank wasn't derailed by Ukraine (on the 30th) choosing to abstain from voting (Ukraine refused to attend); however, the initiative was certainly hampered, with most people on this planet imagining that the occupied Ukrainians would support another tribe who claim to be occupied and terrorized.

The vote on the 30th, which would determine whether or not the International Court of Justice in the Hague would be given a mandate to give their verdict in regards to the occupied territories, resulted in eighty-seven nations supporting the Palestinians, twenty-four nations supporting the Israelis and fifty-three fence-sitting nations (including Ukraine) choosing to abstain. Those who abstained in this instance are clearly not pro-Israel or pro-USA but due to multiple reasons (especially self-defence) chose to remain silent.

The true verdict is 140 vs. 24—because it is hard to understand, tolerate or forgive occupation, and the Palestinians are certainly the 'underdog', which is why they continually receive so much international support.

Perhaps if Hamas had returned to terror and violence the week before the vote, the results would have been markedly different, but as it stands, the majority of the world disagrees with the position of the USA and Israel, including Ukraine.

But why did Ukraine switch her position? Considering that at 'committee stage', she voted in favour of the same initiative in the past, what has changed?

If the 2014 revolution and later civil war and later neighbours war (in Ukraine) had never occurred, without a shadow of a doubt Ukraine would have voted against Israel.

What Ukraine needs in 2023 is demilitarisation and peace, but what she thinks she needs (which is understandable and hard to criticize) is many, many, many, many new weapons of death and destruction to 'throw off' the occupier. Occupied Ukraine has become akin to the occupied West Bank, whose people have for decades sought the help and support of others, and weapons.

It is in this moment of immense stress and calamity in Ukraine that she has felt it necessary to turn her back on the principles, ethics and beliefs she once held because now Ukraine pursues only war (hoping to create peace by war).

This situation is aggravated by the fact that the USA supports Israel but not Palestine and claims to support Ukraine but not Russia. Israel repeatedly requested that Ukraine vote in favour of Israel (understandable), the USA also pressured Ukraine to vote in favour of Israel, which would mean voting against the occupied Palestinians.

Multiple reports claim Ukraine attempted to 'bargain' with Israel immediately prior to the UN vote, which some have termed 'blackmail'—especially very Conservative pro-Israel voices in the USA.

The claim is that Ukraine offered to help to 'support the occupation of the West Bank' (by voting against the resolution) in exchange for the weapons and military supplies Israel has long refused to provide to Ukraine throughout 2022 because Israel doesn't want war with Russia, because no sane person wants war with Russia or with Ukraine because these peoples are strong.

Israel has been fence-sitting in regards to providing military assistance. Ukraine hoped this position would shift in exchange for 'a favour'.

Are many of those who voted against Israel anti-Semitic or envious of Israel/the USA and biased? Yes, of course. Many hate success and strength or that which is different.

Are many of those who voted against Israel (which is, in effect, a vote against the USA due to the de facto union that nation has with Israel) afraid and angered by American expansionism, colonisation, military occupation and political and financial domination? Yes, the USA casts a vast shadow, which is the cause of ire, frustration and consternation everywhere.

There were (in this instance) ethical reasons for voting, emotional reasons for voting, pragmatic reasons for voting, ideological reasons for voting and fear-driven reasons for voting one way or another—in defence of Israel or in defence of the occupied Palestinians. The strong showing of support for those who are occupied suggests the press about the occupied Ukrainians has influenced the end result of the vote—quite possibly the support for Israel would have been greater if Ukraine was not currently locking horns with Russia.

If Ukraine had voted in favour of the resolution two days ago (30/12/2022) one would imagine she would do so to show solidarity with a fellow occupied people.

If Ukraine had voted against the resolution (as Israel/the USA insisted) one would imagine that Ukraine was only angered by Ukrainians being occupied.

But Ukraine did not vote for or against—instead, she didn't attend the vote, which Israel termed, 'Disappointing.'

What this means is Ukraine's international ethics and principles and commitments (during times of war and great desperation and stress) are 'negotiable', something that shouldn't come as a shock to anyone who knows politics. Yet this will come as a shock to the Westerners who wave Ukrainian flags and shout, 'Free Ukraine!' who previously also waved Palestinian flags and shouted, 'Free Palestine!'

If Israel had helped to kill Russians by sending Israeli bullets and bombs to Kiev (no amount of weapons in Ukraine could ever ensure peace—see the chapter 'Nuclear Ukraine') it would mean that she supported certain occupied peoples and was indifferent to Russians being hurt or killed.

The end result of this situation (Ukraine refusing to attend the vote at the UN) is as follows:

Israel is angered.

The USA is angered.

Palestinians are angered.

The Muslim world is angered.

Many Ukrainians are angered because Israel doesn't support Ukraine militarily and the Palestinians are a fellow occupied people.

All of this anger is toxic and will be the cause of more and more people and nations withdrawing their support from Ukraine. Not voting one way or the other hasn't helped the cause of peace in Ukraine; rather, it will be the cause of future diplomatic rifts between Ukraine and the rest of the world.

Why does Israel continually court America and develop ever greater ties with that nation? Dependency and self-defence.

Why does Ukraine continually court America and develop ever greater ties with that nation? Dependency and self-defence.

Without the USA (and her decades of support and aid) would Israel exist in 2023? Without the USA would Ukraine exist in 2023? Possibly not, or at least not in their present conditions.

Once the powerful USA (who are quick to use agent orange or nuclear weapons or torture as a means to maintain international supremacy) offers you protection, your enemies are filled with dread and a sense of foreboding, knowing that you must walk on eggshells and 'follow orders' in order to remain alive, free and sovereign.

Being friends with the USA may ensure your survival (in the case of Israel, for instance), yet if your enemy is already an enemy of the USA and NATO (as in the case of Russia), choosing to ally yourself with the USA will have the end result of painting a rather large target on your back.

Ukraine invited Russia's enemy to live in Ukraine when she requested membership of NATO (which is akin to becoming a new American state, due to that alliance being dominated by America) and must have known Russia would react badly, rather than meekly.

What Ukraine was seeking by insisting on admission to NATO was, in effect, to become the 51st state of America because American soldiers and airmen, marines and sailors would instantly establish military bases throughout the territory of Ukraine and such installations would exist there forever (as in the case of Germany, Korea and Japan) creating eternal dependency and a very real sense of occupation—due to most Ukrainians wishing to protect their homes and communities themselves and desiring full autonomy, self-determination and sovereignty.

Why would America be so benevolent as to protect Ukraine and Ukrainians, risking the death of their servicemen and women at a huge cost to the American taxpayer, without expecting anything in return? She wouldn't.

America desires Ukrainians to love America, to replicate America, to forever tolerate and accommodate hundreds of thousands of American soldiers in Ukraine, to become a dependent nation and to eventually (like in the case of the Southern states and Hawaii) salute their flag, salute their union and to 'become' Americans—becoming their 51st state.

In the case of Israel, if she became the 52nd state of America, it would solve many problems in the Middle East whilst, of course, causing others. Yet, the issue of the Palestinians and their identity and sovereignty (if Israel and Palestine 'became' parts of America) would be addressed and solved almost immediately because everyone in Israel and Palestine would be an American first, with both sides being compelled to live side by side in peace under one American flag with an extra few stars added.

If Ukraine chose a similar route, if she chose to (or was compelled to) become the 51st state, the internal rifts, tribalism and sectarianism would be "solved" via harmonisation, huge welfare and the expansion of the state and state power. Where there is conformity there is peace even if there is no joy, freedom or individuality.

If Ukraine and Israel were US states (many in these nations would welcome this) it would change the balance of world power. Ukraine would then be the USA; the USA would be Russia's neighbour to the west and to the east—a suffocating and untenable situation for Russia, who doesn't wish to watch on whilst being outmanoeuvred, outflanked and surrounded by the USA.

Would Ukraine being a US state have prevented the current conflict in Ukraine? Perhaps, due to Russia being unable to invade nations with nuclear weapons due to such actions being suicidal for both sides. However, in order for Ukraine to become a US state she would first require NATO membership, which she attempted to secure, which would have been the first step to 'becoming Americans'. Russia knew the only way to prevent this situation was to invade Ukraine as threats alone were not deterring Ukraine from pursuing her goals: Becoming a member of NATO and a member of the EU.

If Russia had supported Ukraine's attempt to join NATO (which would mean becoming friends with the USA) Russia would know for a certainty that she could never have a small regional conflict again with Ukraine, that if relations ever became strained between the neighbours the end result (once diplomacy failed) would have to be nuclear war—due to NATO having nuclear weapons and America having nuclear weapons, which would be located in Kiev, which would be pointed at Moscow.

Russia believes that she has chosen the lesser of two evils by engaging in a non-nuclear, non-chemical and non-biological war against the Ukrainian state, knowing that if the USA came to Ukraine (if she became a NATO member or the 51st state) she would be forced to use every weapon in her arsenal to protect against colonisation, humiliation, domination, capitulation and destruction.

It should be known that Ukraine is only willing to allow foreign military bases to be located within her sovereign borders (something America, Russia and China, for instance, would never permit under any circumstances) due to the existence of Russia. If Russia didn't exist, would Ukraine wish to be a member of NATO or the EU? Possibly not.

Ukraine's position on NATO and surrendering sovereignty to the USA and the EU is a fear-driven and reactionary position because if Russia didn't exist, why would Ukraine want American soldiers to come to Kiev? She wouldn't, unless she was a masochist, because only Ukrainians should defend Ukraine, only Russians should defend Russia, only Germans should defend Germany and only Americans should defend America because freedom requires self-sufficiency and self-determination, which means men who intend to remain free will always insist on defending themselves whereas the man who wishes to be dependent on others (a voluntary slave) will beg others to protect him. They will then remain in his territory after being his "saviour" due to having little to no respect for he who chooses security in exchange for occupation.

'Those who would give up essential Liberty, to purchase a little temporary Safety, deserve neither Liberty nor Safety.'
— Benjamin Franklin, 1755.

Ironically, if Ukraine had 6,000 nuclear weapons and Russia had no nuclear weapons (a complete reversal), it would be Russia today who was desperately applying for NATO and EU membership and it would be Ukraine who would be doing everything within her power to prevent such things from occurring, by military intervention if necessary, to ensure long-term survival and protection.

Chapter Twelve — Pour Nuclear Waste into Nuclear Bunkers—It's Meant to Be

(Originally chapter Sixty, from the book *Make America United Again: The Trump-Harris Co-Presidency 2024 – 2028*)

There are many ways to end all human life, many ways to destroy all nations and civilisation; yet there are many ways to save humanity also, many ways to keep nations alive and kicking, with filling in every bunker, in every land, as all embrace honour and courage as we face down and conquer fear and hate, very high up there on the list of ways to save humanity, ways to prevent WWIII.

'We will go down with this ship if enemies come. We do not wish to be here without you, which is why we are filling in our nuclear bunkers,' is what two brave Co-Presidents might jointly announce as the statement is delivered to the American people as well as the international community of nations and peoples. This will signal that the world is about to head in a new direction, with the USA and her people again leading the way and setting the example to follow.

Why does China have aircraft carriers and nuclear ICBMs? Because the USA constructed these things first.

Why do China and Russia and the DPRK have nuclear bunkers buried deep underground? Because the USA built nuclear bunkers first and everyone else followed their lead.

But does it have to be this way? And are these bunkers the things that keep civilisation and humanity and civility alive and ticking over?

Or are bunkers in fact the things that will guarantee that NBC (nuclear, biological or chemical) attacks will take place over the continental United States within the next twenty-four to forty-eight months at the current rate of deterioration of international relations, peace and order?

If one or two US presidents declared that no longer will new bunkers be built in the USA, other nations would follow suit for a whole host of reasons. Beyond the high costs and no citizens considering political or military leadership valid after spending a decade underground avoiding the consequences of their actions, no more bunkers would be constructed due to that act being considered an act of war, or, at the very least, a prelude to war.

Gone be the bunkers, gone be the fear as the leader who knows he will safely live until 100 if he so chooses (by virtue of him having an escape tunnel leading to a bunker) is likely to incite or even start wars if he will soon be impeached or will lose the next election by a huge, embarrassing margin….

Hitler knew he was protected throughout WWII (by bunkers), which ensured the horrors of that conflict continued, just as Pope Clement VII only joined the League of Cognac alliance (which led to Rome being sacked in 1527) as a result of knowing of a tunnel leading to the fortress of Castel Sant'Angelo, which served to save his life when all others around him lost theirs, with the population of Rome falling to a low point of 20,000 after it was sacked by those angered by his posturing and military alliances and edicts.

Remove the bunker; remove the bombast and defiance, incitement and aggression.

If a US president, a UK prime minister, an Israeli prime minister and a Russian president know that declaring war will guarantee that they and every member of their family will die, will they declare war? No.

If all such folk have their friends and family with them (above ground, not in a bunker) in the moment they consider 'pushing the button', they will think twice if the bunker that was previously beneath their feet, which had been filled with ten years' worth of supplies, which could withstand a nuclear strike, was suddenly filled with surplus nuclear waste and topped with tons of the hardest concrete, reinforced with metal rebar, and rendered inoperable for an eternity. Will the button be pushed? No.

We must allow representatives to serve the people; yes, we must allow leaders to lead, but bunkers should play no role in either representing the people or leading the people.

One does not lead in a bunker; one hides and saves his own skin.

Retreating to a bunker is failure and due to the existence of bunkers, the failure is near certain, almost fated to happen again and again and again as history continues to sadly repeat itself.

Clements' secret escape tunnels were built long before he fled the Vatican; Hitler's bunkers were built long before the Red Army stormed into Berlin, and the bunkers being built in this very hour in China, the US, India, Pakistan, the UK, Russia and every other nation are similarly being built long before the next war, which will be the war to end all wars, a cataclysm like no other and one that can only take place if bunkers exist. Please think about this.

Survival, universal survival, is guaranteed not by the existence of bunkers but by their immediate destruction!

Fill them in with toxic waste, nuclear waste and dismantled and inert nuclear warheads. Then pour in the concrete. Be done with bunkers as they give men at their wits' end itchy trigger fingers.

What a brave and bold first move for the first Co-Presidents, the retirement of nuclear bunkers; how honourable and epic and courageous that would be, how such a move would bring all folk together.

Overnight, military budgets worldwide would dramatically shrink as cement trucks were observed in all nations driving out to classified locations as they poured thousands of tons of concrete into the dastardly holes in the ground and in mountains and in every other place where some folk seek to exist in peace and harmony whilst their countrymen suffer above, leaderless, abandoned, betrayed.

Fill in the bunkers. Be brave; be honourable; be human.

And if this advice is ignored, just know that six months after the nuclear war you failed to avert, when you feel safe and secure in your hole in the ground, as you observe throngs of your people outside seemingly fruitlessly attempting to break in, do not laugh at them, thinking them all wasting their time and energy due to your underground fortress being impenetrable, because they will not be trying to break in to steal your supplies, no. They are outside for a completely different reason—they are sealing you in, blocking all escape hatches. They are entombing pharaoh because they know that if they release him/her, and the assorted scientists and politicians and military officers who dwell therein, history will repeat itself eventually.

Do not expect things to be the same afterwards, after you kill your nation then run away. Those bunkers shall be your tombs.

Chapter Thirteen — The Chief Negotiator

(Originally chapter Thirty-Three from the book, *How We Will Create Peace in Ukraine and the World*)

I am the chief negotiator for Ukraine in this scenario, with peace negotiations taking place in a small conference room in Ankara, in the very near future.

The chief negotiator for the Russian side may appear serious and stoic, his demeanour defensive, even brash. *Yet once upon a time*, I think to myself, *he cried until his mother took out one of her breasts to nurture her creation, her most prized possession.*

I do not see a threat when I look at the chief negotiator for Russia, I see the child he once was, but I know that, eventually, when one day he cried out for the breast, it was denied to him because his mother instinctively knew the coddling had to end in order to make him stronger, even though it broke her heart. I know he was forever changed by that event, just as I know he was forever changed by being forced to attend school, just as puberty and heartbreaks and rejections also fundamentally changed that once small and helpless child.

I notice his wedding ring, I remember reading that he had two children and I think to myself, *I'm someone's child also, and I would hate it if anyone felt anger towards my parents in the same way I have been told I should feel anger towards this parent, this Russian, this man, this human.*

I know that he has suffered, because we all do, and when looking at him I find myself wishing his suffering was lesser than mine, or at least no worse, before our paths met in Ankara.

I look at him again and I see a child in need of nurture, no different from myself.

I see a child crying out, desperately afraid of becoming the cause of the apocalypse, needing nurture, reassurance and love.

I break protocol.

I approach the chief negotiator for Russia and request that he stands up and faces me; he does so. We stand close enough to touch each other.

I ask him to close his eyes as I close my eyes for one minute; he agrees.

I then tell him he should silently ask himself a question as he begins to see my face again, and if the answer to the question is 'happy' we should hug, but if his answer is 'sad', we should retake our seats instead and continue being rivals rather than friends.

I tell him the question as our eyes remain closed.

'Will you be happy if when you open your eyes you can see me, which proves I wasn't killed last night when a missile hit my hotel in Kiev, or would you be sad if when you open your eyes, you see me here, standing before you, having survived that attack? We have never met each other before. I am Ukrainian; you are Russian, I am told we are enemies. So tell me, will it make you happy or sad if you see that I am still alive when you open your eyes?'

We open our eyes at the same time.

'Happy, I am happy that you are standing before me, brother,' the Russian chief negotiator tells me.

'I feel the same, I am happy that you are still standing before me, I am glad that you still live!' I tell him before we firmly hug whilst taking unusually large and slow breaths, our bodies communicating calmness to each other, our nerves and anxieties being soothed in a nano-second, with us both thinking in the same moment, *The Brotherhood of Man trumps everything!* as the two of us spiritually merge into one.

I tell him about how I think we could make peace, even the most far-fetched ideas, and ask him to share all of his ideas also because we instinctively know that if we work together as objective individuals who love people but hate war, we will easily have achieved peace before lunch.

Is this a wildly optimistic prospect? Yes, but that's a good thing because pessimism and apathy are getting us absolutely nowhere, only wild optimism and profound empathy, renewed strength and mutual respect stand any chance of averting the end of everything.

Hugs, not bayonets.

Chapter Fourteen — The UN, NGOs and Foreign Aid

It is easy and fulfilling to virtue signal, especially for compassionate narcissists, by attaching yourself to an underdog or perceived underdog of your choice.

It is fun and exciting to adorn yourself perhaps in an 'Arafat scarf' as you believe you are some sort of hero; yet, to get to the anti-Israel demonstration billed as a pro-Palestinian demonstration, to get to the airport in order to fly to Gaza to deliver aid there, you do realise, don't you, that you first have to step over your own homeless folk? You have to walk past your own suffering and needy people as you choose to attach yourselves to the dramatic and loud conflict affecting complete strangers. We should all get our own houses in order first before we transfer the contents of our bank accounts and our hearts abroad.

All manner of radicals and professional protesters, protestors for life, and career complainers and those who never wish to work for a living are found dwelling within NGOs and aid agencies, which are frequently found to engage in criminality as in the case of the UNRWA, who acknowledge that many members of Hamas worked for them, were paid by them and were involved in the October 7th attack including a Hamas commander in Lebanon who was killed last month in an Israeli strike who was later found to have worked for the UNRWA. Another top commander, who was killed in Gaza last week, also moonlighted as a UN aid worker. The UNRWA has subsequently confirmed both men had been employees.

And the problems at the UN in regards to Israel extend far beyond the UNHRC as I learn today from the reporting of Luke Tress in the *Times of Israel* who shared the shocking fact that, in 2022, the UN condemned Israel more than all other countries combined, with the UN General Assembly introducing fifteen anti-Israel measures in comparison to introducing thirteen against the rest of the world.

Further, since 2015 the UN has adopted 140 resolutions criticizing Israel whilst during that same period passing only sixty-eight resolutions against all other countries combined, which seems like favouritism, which seems like deep bias. I have no dog in this fight, yet it appears the UN is being used to 'bash Israel' and to demoralise and bully her. I imagine, in large part, these relentless attacks are being launched in the direction of

Jerusalem as a result of the presence of Jewish folk in the Middle East in addition to Israel being a democracy; these are the two apparent "sins" being committed that so irk a large cohesive voting bloc at the UN, to that institution's shame.

You cannot vote Israel out of existence; these are hollow, fleeting victories, gnats biting at Israel. All those resolutions are pinpricks and irksome, annoying Israel; they achieve cheap catharsis and little else and they certainly do not create the conditions necessary for true long-lasting peace in the Middle East, which should be our collective common goal.

I understand many wishing to hurt Israel to get "justice" for Palestinians. I understand this, but I know this is not the way to reach Israel and to create peace. We must stop lashing out at the Jewish state; that is the start of wisdom and peace.

Stop taking cheap shots at Israel, invite her to peace conferences instead; respect her and her right to exist and we can begin moving in a new direction, one that does not see the UN become irrelevant due to it coming to be but a vehicle for anti-Semitism and anti-Israel actions and bullying. The facts speak for themselves, 140 resolutions passed against a Jewish democracy and sixty-eight in the same time period passed against every other nation combined.

The Jew is very much the scapegoat for a great many nations, attacked not only at the UN but also by NGOs and their representatives and international supporters who consistently have been shown to take sides in the cold war between Israel and her neighbours in the Middle East.

In the eye-opening book *Escaping the Cult of Guilt: The Dark Side of Charity and NGOs* I make the case for defunding NGOs and aid agencies for a whole host of sensible reasons. I suggest that, at a minimum, their tax status should be changed as well as their ability to inject deeply graphic and disturbing imagery into the homes and hearts of every living human on the planet; one, due to the psychological harm this causes to especially vulnerable people and to the children who are exposed to the forced sharing of international suffering at the behest of NGOs and aid agencies, and, two, because all too often the "charity appeals" are politically motivated, with a side being taken and the end goal desired being the destruction of democratic nations such as the state of Israel.

The bias of many NGOs, their unethical practices and them being all too often the cause of the extension of suffering and conflicts and never being the facilitators of conflicts ending is more than reason enough to ban NGOs and aid agencies from operating in your nation.

NGOs, in part, are the cause of the conflict being eternally extended, primarily stemming from a result of the activists (almost always paid) seeking to create eternal problems for themselves, never wanting there to be a real and lasting peace as then their vocation and source of income would suddenly be gone.

Chapter Fifteen — Delyo Is ALL OF US

(Originally chapter One Hundred and Four from the book, *How We Will Create Peace in Ukraine and the World*)

My friends, we are so very different yet so very similar. We all need to survive, we all deserve to survive; but survival requires change because at the present time we are racing towards oblivion.

There exists a song of Slavic origin that perfectly sums up our species, which is why it was added to NASA's 'Golden record'.

'Izlel ye Delyo Haydutin', from the original Bulgarian Излел е Дельо хайдутин, which translates to, 'Delyo has become a Hajduk' (hajduk = rebel or freedom fighter).

Delyo has become hayduk,
the hayduk, the rebel
with the Dumbovi and the Karadjovi clans.
Delyo gave the following orders
to the ayans (local notables) of Zlatograd,
to the brazen-faced governors:

- There are two aunts of mine in the village.
Do not make them Turks (= do not convert them to Islam),
do not besmirch them,
because when I come back
a lot of mothers will cry,
a lot of young brides.

Gyulsume told Delyo:

- Beware, Delyo, beware,
you are being threatened, Delyo
the Zlatograd rulers,
the brazen-faced governors,
they cast a silver bullet

for you, Delyo, to kill you.

- Gyulsume, my love Gyulsume,
not yet is born a man
who could kill me.

This same song, this story of humanity, our story, is hurtling through interstellar space aboard Voyager 1 at a distance of 23.171 billion km from Earth as of October 20, 2021, the most distant artificial object from our planet.

This song is about the human divide, about sectarianism, about our differences, about being a rebel, about pride, courage, indomitability, honour and resistance to tyranny, about revenge, about murder and about inhumanity. This song was birthed in the Bulgarian Rhodope Mountains in the late 18th century yet could have been birthed in 2023 in any number of nations.

Delyo was born in Belovidovo (today Zlatograd) in the Smolyan region in the 17th century. He headed an armed detachment of rebels in the central Rhodopes and acted against the Ottoman authorities' Islamization of the local Bulgarian population.

In 1720, he led a group of united rebel detachments that attacked Raykovo (today a neighbourhood of Smolyan) in revenge for the murder of 200 locals who refused to convert from Christianity to Islam.

Delyo could have been a native American rebel fighting against Anglo Saxon Christians; he could have been a Muslim in the Middle East fighting back the crusading Christians; he could have been a Christian Spaniard fighting against the Moorish Muslim invasion of Spain; he could have been a pagan rebel in England fighting against Christians; he could have been a Christian Englishman fighting back the pagan Vikings—Delyo is ALL OF US! Delyo is ALL OF US! Delyo is ALL OF US!

When we realise this, when we accept this fundamental truth, we will be at peace. All good men have the propensity for great good and great evil simultaneously; there are no saints among our number, only sinners to be. There is equality in this, our nature is the same, our instincts the same, our insistence on eternal survival the same, even if it requires barbarism.

When NASA added this beautiful yet tragic folk song to the golden record, consciously or subconsciously, they were asking for help, humbly broadcasting this song, which describes humanity's bane.

NASA was saying to potential aliens, 'We want to grow and evolve, but we don't know how. We are warlike and dangerous, prideful and tribal, please teach us the lessons you must have learnt in order to have survived long enough to have been able to colonise the stars. Teach us, we beseech you.'

What incredible humility. Broadcasting that song was admitting our faults, total honesty, because we can never have peace whilst secrecy and lies remain and whilst we remain in denial about the fact that we all have the propensity to be Deylo as well as to become those he fought so courageously against.

Russians, imagine you were born in India, imagine you are Hindu Indians grateful that the British Empire has left your ancestral lands. Would you not support the Ukrainian underdog in 2023?

Ukrainians, imagine you were an ethnic Russian, born to Russian parents in the Donbas who observed the 2014 Maidan protests in horror as anti-Russian sentiment spread following the EU and NATO-approved coup, as your identity, language, culture and heritage looked doomed due to the sudden expected influx of the EU and NATO (the USA) coming to Donbas as soon as possible....

Russians, Ukrainians, please try to imagine walking in one another's shoes.

Do not do this for yourself, do this for your children, for your nephews, for your grandchildren, for the future of our amazing species, which deserves to survive. What a marvel we are, what a jewel we are, what amazing things we can achieve. We can rise; we can evolve. I know we have the strength to overcome these obstacles and knock down the hurdles that slow our progress to a crawl.

No more arms races, no more space race, no more nuclear weapons—we can do this, we can all win, we do not have to jump off the ledge, we can choose a new path instead. We can survive, we must survive, we will survive, because we are all Delyo but we are all Gandhi also. We are are all Jesus and we are all Mohammad and Oppenheimer also because we are human, because we are one and the spark of creation dells within us all! Leadership/stewardship of the tribe may fall to any one of us, at any time, nature knows this; nature has faith in us all. There are abilities and degrees of tolerance and compassion and inner sacrifice that lie dormant until they are needed.

This is the moment; this is the moment for all to become actively engaged in the survival of the tribes. All must lead, all must demand responsibilities and duty and purpose. Stop hiding in the shadows, this is the moment right here, this is your time.

'Delyo has become a Hajduk' is most famously sung by the folk singer Valya Balkanska, her surname means 'of the Balkans' where Delyo was also birthed; her 1977 recording is included on the Golden Record carried on board the Voyager 1 and Voyager 2 probes, it is hard to listen to her rendition without feeling deep sorrow for humanity yet deep love and pride also.

We are amazing; we are terrible; we are everything else in between—we are humans.

Conclusion

Is the Saudi Proposal too ambitious, 'too big', for Saudi Arabia?

Doesn't Iran want to attempt any and every solution to ending the cold war in the Middle East, even if that means enacting the brave resettlement plan?

Do we really prefer nihilistic descent into regional war precipitating WWIII as a preference to the eternal existence of the State of Israel?

Are the plans offered within this book so much worse than nuclear annihilation?

Keep asking questions, keep searching for the right and honest answers and through this you will discover the correct course of action, the correct dispassionate course of action that will birth glorious peace and a proud new chapter for all parties involved—the air raid shelters in Israel should not be there forever, just as the refugee camps should not, and will not, exist forever.

***

Did Israel 'do wrong' after the October 7th attacks?

Many folk, even some Israelis and members of the international Jewish diaspora will answer 'yes'.

However, what would you have the State of Israel do following such an attack?

Paris is struck by paragliders and militants; hundreds are kidnapped, indiscriminately so; men, women and children, civilians stolen away from Paris and many murdered.

Would you expect the French to sit on their hands and do nothing?

Would you expect the French to 'ask permission' of the UN, of NGOs and of assorted long-time French-haters for permission to respond, for permission to search out the kidnapped French citizens whilst seeking to eliminate the militants involved in the brazen attack? Is that what would be expected?

On October 7th, the tactics used were aggression and terror and dominance and fear and bombast; this guaranteed the Israeli response being aggressive, full of terror and dominance and fear and bombast—just as it was in the 'shock and awe' campaign in Iraq, with Saddam Hussein ruling with an iron fist for many decades, the Americans knowing that only the projection of massive strength and dominance would win the day.

The October 7th attack was not committed to "highlight legitimate complaints" as if you desire compensation from a man, you do not rape and kidnap his child and kill his brother because that will not result in you being awarded compensation, no; rather, the man who may have wronged you long ago now seeks immediate revenge and retribution and justice himself.

October 7th cannot be justified. Nothing can justify that attack, nor can you justify the deliberate targeting of civilians.

If you state, 'Israel did wrong after October 7th, they reacted in the wrong way, I wanted them to react differently,' I ask how did you want them to react and why did you not email Jerusalem with your "orders" ahead of time?

There are no puppet strings on Israel; it is the Jewish state, the one and only Jewish state. She stands alone in the desert fighting for her existence; she is not subject to the will of others but to the will of her people.

Would you have had Israel do nothing? Not try to rescue their hostages, their brothers and sisters and sons and daughters? Did you want Israel to apologise for being attacked and violated and shamed and wronged and harmed? Did you want Israel to suddenly surrender completely without firing a bullet or a missile, without throwing her flesh at her foe in a desperate attempt to search through those tunnels for their family members and fellow citizens whom they deeply love and cherish? Is that what you wanted, what you desired?

Every sane nation would have responded in the same way Israel responded.

Look at the response to Pearl Harbour; look at the response to Nazi aggression in WWII.

States always fight fire with fire, yet importantly, very importantly, America never wanted to drop those bombs, just as Israel never wanted to launch the massive counteroffensive in Gaza.

Israel did not want to hurt Palestinians and Israel does not want to hurt Palestinians, proven by the fact that immediately prior to October 7th Israeli-Saudi relations were improving, setting the scene for great diplomacy and trade and cooperation and beautiful lasting peace … which Jerusalem knew would be scuppered upon the occasion of future Israeli clashes with Hamas and the Palestinian people. Understand that Israel knew the peace with Saudi Arabia meant the beginning of the end of the Middle Eastern cold war and a final peaceful resolution in Palestine/Gaza.

Israel never wanted to attack Gaza in 2024, just as no one wanted to attack Hiroshima, Nagasaki or Dresden.

Israel is not some one-dimdensional sadistic beast who relishes hurting vulnerable and innocent people; she is a hopeful democracy made up of history's most unlikely survivors who broke their backs and swallowed much pride attempting to forge a good alliance with Saudi Arabia immediately prior to the Hamas attack last October. Israel was seeking to build bridges. Please allow her now to continue where she left off as the alternative is bleak pointless war and tumult.

Would I have preferred it if only soldiers/fighters in Gaza had been killed in the justifiable Israeli counterattack? Of course! Yet that, although attempted, was impossible as Israel desperately attempted to defeat the threat whilst recovering her children.

Some are passive and indifferent perhaps when their loved ones are killed or kidnapped. Israel is not of that number.

The tragic civilian deaths (especially of children) only occurred due to the October 7th attack, all can agree on this.

If the October 7th attack by Hamas had not occurred, today all of the innocents who died as a result of the urban combat and strikes against Hamas would all be alive and the buildings and infrastructure now reduced to rubble would still be standing and in good order.

The way to guarantee an end to Nazism is to hit Berlin hard and to hit Dresden hard and thereafter occupy the entire nation for decades, the alternative being to bear witness to the Third Reich regrouping and rising again a few short years later, only to drag Europe into another pointless war of destruction and hate.

Civilians get caught in the crossfire, but only when the white flag is not raised.

When Japan surrendered, civilians were immediately safe.

When Germany surrendered, civilians were immediately safe.

And it is the logical Israeli belief that when Hamas surrenders or vacates (given, of course, safe passage), Palestinian civilians will become immediately safe, which is what we all desire deeply.

***

Sociopathy and psychopathy are burgeoning as a result of the ongoing conflict with the terror felt on both sides causing young people to become emotionally numb and detached, antisocial, and in that climate, made worse by endless fear, armed groups everywhere and constant instability and so much time spent in air raid shelters, sociopathy becomes hugely multiplied, setting the scene for trouble ahead for the other side but also for the individuals' family and community also.

Israel is a powerful and well-funded state, yet, even so, sociopathy is on the rise as a result of the tumult and fear consuming her, with individual acts of aggression from Israel's defenders having their foundation in childhoods spent cowering in bunkers or terrified when playing in the park when men appeared armed with knives or with suicide vests strapped to them. And if the pain and fear and terror and isolation and detachment can affect Israelis, of course it is a far greater curse upon the Palestinian people who do not have the same level of support for those with mental illness/disorders/PTSD.

And it is the sociopathy infused with nihilism and the weaponising of the psychopathic and sociopathic minority among the Palestinian people that of course enables the extension of the violent conflict and facilitates every attack against Israelis, especially against civilians.

Ordinarily, in peace time, those who are considered "heroes" today by Israel haters in Gaza who engaged in the kidnappings and killings in recent times would be deemed by their own government and representatives and mental health professionals to be 'too dangerous to be at liberty'. It is only due to the fact that 'the wolf is at the door' that those born with psychopathy within them and those who due to circumstance and nurture have become sociopathic are at liberty in this hour and among Gaza's/Palestine's leadership and military and who seemingly have also infiltrated aid agencies and NGOs.

A suddenly free and autonomous and demilitarised Gaza/Palestine would place most folk associated with Hamas into rehabilitation or psychiatric wards if not prison. The mentally unwell, those harmed by trauma, PTSD and made sociopathic, are being used in this hour to inflict hurt upon Israel. But make no mistake; the second the fighting ends, these folk will not be deemed heroes or saviours by the Palestinians but dangerous criminals within a peaceful and well-ordered and democratic and anti-corrupt society.

***

The existence of refugee camps anywhere on Earth is disturbing, upsetting and plain unrighteous as folk cannot be free, cannot be natural, cannot be themselves and cannot achieve anything close to self-actualisation or harmony, love or joy in such places.

Men need to be free, as do women, as do children.

I desire not to give Israel a punch on the nose as most do who march against her, who call her names and who oftentimes unwittingly come to support militant groups, unwittingly come to fund those same groups and who unwittingly or not come to be aligned with groups as well as states that truly desire a genocidal solution in the Middle East.

Punching Israel's nose achieves nothing other than making us feel better in places such as the UK and the USA after witnessing shocking imagery coming out of the refugee camps and out of Gaza.

We see the young there are helpless, which makes us feel helpless and then ashamed of ourselves if we are caring and empathic and loving if we do not intervene, if we do not throw ourselves at the state of Israel, if we do not dash ourselves against Israel, if we do not assail her, even fund radical murderous groups, so long as some hurt is inflicted upon Israel.

I understand the anger and frustration and it is good people most of the time in the West who direct anger in the direction of Israel, and these same good people, if they wish for the pain and hurt to be removed from their hearts, need to do something they perhaps believe impossible; they need to remove the emotion and passion they feel in regards to Israel, the IDF and the human tragedy that is the refugee camps and the appearance of apartheid as the intense emotions and the immersion in the suffering of Palestinians does not aid the intervention, it does not help or save Palestinians.

Caring so much about one set of folk whilst considering the other side little more than the Borg, rather than scared, fragile and equally vulnerable humans, only extends the pain and suffering and bloodshed and discord.

As impossible as it seems, those committed to 'battling Israel forever' to get justice for Palestine and the Palestinians and for the folk in the camps and for the innocent victims caught up in this soon-to-end conflict need to become dispassionate when working to save those they claim to care about most dearly of all, not forever but long enough for your involvement to bear good, peaceful fruit, my friends.

An easy way to achieve this stoic and self-disciplined psychological state that will ensure the conflict ends in three months rather than after an additional three long and fraught decades is to imagine that in London, in Berlin, in Washington DC, in Paris and in Quebec there are suddenly dozens of refugee camps as that will be the end result for a certainty if the intense emotions and rhetoric and unwise Western support for one side of the conflict long continues.

If the Middle East, emboldened by anti-Israel sentiment at the UN, emboldened and raised up by NGO support and by sympathetic liberal and caring Western support decide it is time to unite together against Israel, using Gaza as a cynical excuse, as a justification for the unilateral all-out assault on Israel, it will mean WWIII is just around the corner, at which point, Western readers who are surrounded by privilege and excess in their respective nations and good order with no refugee camps present will immediately bear witness to refugee camps springing up everywhere following the inevitable nuclear war that will follow.

The Palestinian people do not desire war; they desire and deserve peace.

We must face reality, we must accept the truth, and we must prevent ourselves from seeking to bully the State of Israel into compliance because the images and videos we have witnessed coming out of Gaza are harrowing and cause us to become distraught and full of rage.

The Jewish people do not desire war, they desire and deserve peace, and their remarkable democracy and proven anti-corruption credentials are an epic achievement in the region, and make no mistake, there are many Jews who feel the pain of the Palestinians, who need the conflict to be brought to an end hurriedly in the interests of their own mental health.

There is no evil, hate-filled Nazi beast in Tel Aviv and Jerusalem seeking to consume and burn and eternally terrorise unarmed civilians of another race, no. In fact, just the other day, an Arab Israeli soldier by the name of Muhammad died in the defence of the state of Israel. Those who hate stateism, those who abhor order, those who despise everything that is not Islam and Muslim and everyone who viscerally hates democracy hates Israel as she is a state that desires order; she is quarrelling with people who follow the words of the Quran and she is also a democracy.

This fact is the cause of so much suffering for Israel, which in turn is passed on to Palestine and the Palestinians.

Every man and his dog who hates democracy can 'beat up on Israel' and call for that state to be destroyed citing all sorts of historical reasons and previous borders as to why Israel should not exist, with these same people however not wishing to revert the borders in Cyprus, in southern Serbia/Kosovo or the borders in the heart of Europe that were dramatically changed not all that long ago in the interests of creating long-term peace and stability.

Every man and his dog who hates states, the anarchists, the neo-Marxists and the "citizens of the world" sees a punching bag in Israel and can justify their hate and anger and bullying because she is seemingly "in the wrong" in regards to the Palestinians.

Every Muslim and every "Muslim ally" who desires an entirely Muslim world sees Palestinian suffering as an excuse, as a springboard to enable the implementation of a new global Islamic caliphate.

Half of the time the "pro-Palestine" demonstrations and marches are in fact a prelude to an international culture war, one that would involve radical leftists and Islam, just as the grandfather of Woke, William Quilliam, always desired (as evidenced within the book *Wokeism Is Crumbs from the Table of Globalist Elites*) with that Englishman (the first social justice warrior and the creator of cancel culture it should be known) back in the 1890s embracing Islam and the Ottoman Empire. The script now is little different to then; nothing has changed, the thinking is no different. The desire for a monotropistic world, forced equality enabled by a single creed dominating humanity and the world still burns in the hearts of the privileged few.

And then added into this curious alliance of non-democracies in the Middle East – neo-Marxists, most NGOs, Muslim states, radical leftists, democracy haters, one-world desirers and international social justice warriors – are also found neo-Nazis who applaud when Israel is hurt, just as they applaud when Palestinians are hurt whenever Israel returns fire.

What a consortium. What a huge, international and disparate force Israel must contend with daily. What immense pressure is being exerted, which would cause the weak to buckle, to surrender, to run away, to shrink and cower; yet we do not see this from the Jews, which is reason enough to respect them and the Jewish state. They take every attack, be it physical, financial (boycotts, Quilliam style) or merely psychological and in terms of PR as a result of anti-Israel marches and demonstrations without ever faltering or retreating.

Please understand that if all of these combined efforts are not felling Israel, and if the militant and guerrilla actions are not felling her, if all of the hate being directed at her is not felling her, it is the definition of insanity to continue behaving in the same way, to continue using the exact same tactics again and again and again.

I understand that, if you are a part of the consortium of folk and groups listed above, you desire to "win"; yet I suggest you change what you consider to constitute "winning" as currently your every effort results in an ever stronger state of Israel, ever more Israeli patriotism, and ever more friction in the Middle East in tandem with more refugee camps being needed for Palestinians following yet another backlash after suicide bomb attacks, knife attacks, truck attacks or paraglider attacks.

Winning, my friends, is brokering a good and fair peace.

We will not all get what we want, we cannot be permitted to in fact, as some want democracy to end in Israel and the Middle East, some want an Islamic caliphate, some want to 'hang Israeli leaders', some want the annihilation of the ancient and indomitable Jewish people. We cannot get what we want. We must unclench our fists; we must stop looking at the troubling images on TV and the internet, which we know will only increase our radicalism and our internal psychological suffering, which does not aid the Palestinians one iota as all we are doing is stealing their grief. Would you attend random funerals in the UK or New Zealand or Peru and wail and cry and become angered and enraged as a result of that human dying despite not being a relation or friend or knowing them in any capacity whatsoever? No. Why? Because that would be considered by most reasonable folk as insanity and the family and friends of the deceased would insist that you be arrested and thereafter subjected to a rigorous psychiatric evaluation.

Stop immersing yourself in the suffering of others. Stop this perverse masochistic practice that lays you low whilst rendering you a useless ally for the Palestinian people who need level-headed and grown-up and strong friends to aid them in peace negotiations, not those with out-of-control emotions who scream 'cancel, cancel, cancel' and 'boycott, boycott, boycott' every five minutes.

If you truly wish to help, become, for a time at least dispassionate, until we have won a great lasting peace in the Middle East. Be strong for the Palestinian people, which means remaining neutral and, importantly, even tempered, because anger will only lead to war, wars like the Iran/Iraq war, which saw Saudi Arabia bankrolling Iraq as Israel bankrolled Iran and as Iran was intrinsic in aiding Israel in destroying Iraqi nuclear research facilities.

Anger and animosity will encourage new wars; yet, this time, mustard gas will be the least of our worries. Saudis handed out gasmasks to every citizen during the first Gulf War, but gas masks will be of no use in the next cataclysm should it come to the Middle East, and it will come for a certainty if the consortium of anti-Israel forces continues the relentless illogical and ultimately nihilistic attacks that will push us all eventually towards WWIII, unless we devote ourselves to peace, not to recriminations and dwelling on the past and on social justice but peace—pure, good and optimistic and righteous peace.

I respect the Jewish, Iranian, Palestinian, Saudi and all other peoples in this region that has been so bitterly fought over down through the ages. They all deserve respect. None are weak, none are lesser than their neighbours, and I know that Israel respects Iran as Iran respects Israel, as I also know there exists mutual respect among all Middle Eastern states as the cold war there, which together we will bring to a crashing end, has taken a heavy toll on patience and tolerance and willpower.

All of these proud states and peoples have proven their worth and courage time and again, which is why I know their leaders have the strength to hug one another after the good and lasting peace is brokered, as Arafat would have.

Thank you for your time.

The Peace Series

Peace in Ukraine is not a dream; it is soon to be a reality. Peace in the Middle East is not fantasy, it will soon be achieved. Peace between Democrats and Republicans in the USA is just around the corner.

And world peace, once considered impossible, may soon be brokered.

This innovative series of peace-birthing and empathy-multiplying books will spread peace, understanding, education, optimism and hope far and wide whilst reducing sectarianism, hate and needless friction and disputes between neighbours.

Book One How We Will Create Peace in Ukraine and the World
Book Two Five Ways to Create Peace in the Middle East
Book Three Make America United Again: The Trump-Harris Co-Presidency 2024 – 2028
Book Four Plan C: Mutually Assured Survival
Book Five The Far Right and Far Left Are Far from Opposites
Book Six 10 EASY WAYS Russia Could Destroy Germany and the EU in 2025
Book Seven Six Ways to Prevent WWIII

Collectively these unique guides to peace will stimulate debate, warn of the dangers of complete globalization, co-dependency and WWIII, which we can and will avoid, and empower all to aid the cause of peace wherever they live and whatever their individual belief system or world outlook.

When only the few decide the fates of all, tyranny and war arise, whereas when all have access to the facts, when all are enabled to get involved in aiding the cause of peace and justice and equality, the future will look very differently indeed.

These books teach much yet ask much also as it will not be an easy task to save our world and our individual communities and nations; it will require taking on new responsibilities, being courageous, and sacrifices and comprise will be required also.

Yet afterwards, after the winnable and righteous battle for peace has been won, the blissful rewards that follow, the removal of anxiety and terror, the end of conflicts and of hatred and the reinvigoration of optimism and brotherhood will all be worth the struggle and effort.

Peace is just around the corner, and perhaps, just perhaps, the guide to achieving a good and lasting peace might be found within this series of books.

About the Author

Bruce Masters is a British author, psychologist, and optimist, a campaigner for democracy and peace, and a campaigner against globalisation and political and religious extremism.

A prolific author, Masters has written over 50 books spanning multiple genres: political, psychological, self-help and sociological as well as fiction, hoping to improve, educate and inspire.

In addition to being known for his revolutionary Peace Book series (including *Six Ways to Prevent WWIII* and *How We Will Create Peace in Ukraine and the World*) and his Capitalism and Democracy series of books Masters is a leading researcher and writer in the fields of autism, neurodivergence and atypicality. His suite of books relating to these subjects includes *Autistic Jesus, The Führer of Asperg: A New Understanding of Fascism, Autism and the Third Reich, ConjectureMania, The Christ Conspiracy, Tripartheid* and *The Continuation of the Origin of the Species*.

Bruce is a man of many talents and interests: a political observer and analyst, researcher and occasional satirist.

When not writing, he leads a quiet life with his family and is thankful for having the drive, knowledge and will required to birth so many unexpected, empathy-multiplying and thought-provoking political, psychological, and sociological works.

Bruce's books are very much like Marmite: You will either love or hate his unapologetically bombastic and forthright 'tough love' writing style and his leadership-heavy political and social critique and musings.

Yet one thing is for certain; you will not be bored as entertainment in addition to a roller coaster of education intermingled with opinion is guaranteed from beginning to end.

Books by the Author

(Published and coming soon)

The Capitalism and Democracy Book Series:
Book One The Political Lottery — Democracy's Last Best Hope of Survival
Book Two Capitalism Hates You
Book Three The Liberal Loophole Jails: A Peaceful and Righteous Revolution
Book Four The Cancellation of Coronation Street, EastEnders and the National Lottery
Book Five Why Charles Dickens No Longer Loves the White Working Class
Book Six Why The British Stopped Breeding
Book Seven How Nigel Farage Became Prime Minister
Book Eight The Soul Exchange
Book Nine Smartphones are Dumb
Book Ten The M25 Solution — The Creation of the Republic of London

The Peace Series:
Book One How We Will Create Peace in Ukraine and the World
Book Two Five Ways to Create Peace in the Middle East
Book Three Make America United Again: The Trump-Harris Co-Presidency 2024 – 2028
Book Four Plan C: Mutually Assured Survival
Book Five The Far Right and Far Left Are Far from Opposites
Book Six 10 EASY WAYS Russia Could Destroy Germany and the EU in 2025
Book Seven Six Ways to Prevent WWIII

The 33 Essential Questions Series:
Book One The Truth at Last! 33 Essential Questions for Conspiracy Theorists
Book Two The Truth at Last! 33 Essential Questions for Elon Musk
Book Three The Truth at Last! 33 Essential Questions for Prince Harry
Book Four The Truth at Last! 33 Essential Questions for Prince Andrew
Book Five The Truth at Last! 33 Essential Questions for Tommy Robinson
Book Six The Truth at Last! 33 Essential Questions for the Alt-right and

Alt-left
Book Seven The Truth at Last! 33 Essential Questions for Christians

The UnWoke, Anti-Hate, Anti-Guilt Series of Books:
Book One Wokeism Is Crumbs from the Table of Globalist Elites
Book Two Wokeing Kills
Book Three Voluntary Taxation and Capital Punishment: For a Just, Equal and Corruption-Free Society
Book Four Escaping the Cult of Guilt: The Dark Side of Charity and NGOs
Book Five Defeating Fentanyl
Book Six Ending the Migrant Crisis in Europe: Preventing Class Wars, Race Wars and the Destruction of the EU
Book Seven The Sudden and Unexpected Multiculturalisation of Mayfair, Kensington and Belgravia — Which Ended Mass Immigration and White Flight in the UK
Book Eight Globalisation, Mass Immigration, Wokeism and Multiculturalism on Trial (Compilation of Books 1–7)

Psychology/Neurodivergence/Autism:
The Continuation of the Origin of the Species
Autistic Jesus
Don't Judge a Book by Its Cover: 21 Remarkable Similarities Between Donald Trump and Tommy Robinson
The List — The Death of Antisocial Behaviour and Noise Pollution and the Evolution of the Real Estate Industry
The Führer of Asperg: A New Understanding of Fascism, Autism and the Third Reich
Tripartheid
ConjectureMania
The Christ Conspiracy, aka The Rise of the Light Triads
The Truth at Last! 33 Essential Questions for Conspiracy Theorists

Biographical Exposés:
Russell Brand: False Prophet
One Election Please… How J.K. Rowling Bought British Politics, Hid Her True Self and Hoodwinked the World — an Unauthorised Biographical Exposé
The Truth at Last! 33 Essential Questions for Elon Musk
The Truth at Last! 33 Essential Questions for Prince Andrew
The Truth at Last! 33 Essential Questions for Prince Harry

The Truth at Last! 33 Essential Questions for Tommy Robinson

The Rowling Trilogy:
Book One J.K. Rowling In: It's a Kind of Magic
Book Two How Not to Get Sued by J.K. Rowling
Book Three One Election Please… How J.K. Rowling Bought British Politics, Hid Her True Self and Hoodwinked the World — an Unauthorised Biographical Exposé

Bruce Masters' One-Day Book Series:
Plan C: Mutually Assured Survival
The Liberal Loophole Jails: A Peaceful and Righteous Revolution
The American Altruist Assassin
Why The British Stopped Breeding
The List: The Death of Antisocial Behaviour and Noise Pollution — and the Evolution of the Real Estate Industry
Capitalism Hates You
Why Charles Dickens No Longer Loves the White Working Class
The Rule of Ten — How Prince Andrew Came to Be Exiled to Switzerland
The Political Lottery — Democracy's Last Best Hope of Survival

Fiction:
Plan C: Mutually Assured Survival
The Liberal Loophole Jails: A Peaceful and Righteous Revolution
The American Altruist Assassin
The Day Bill Gates Ended Crime
Wokeing Kills
The Sudden and Unexpected Multiculturalisation of Mayfair, Kensington and Belgravia — Which Ended Mass Immigration and White Flight in the UK
J.K. Rowling In: It's a Kind of Magic
The Cancellation of Coronation Street, EastEnders and the National Lottery
The Lord of Purgatory
Adrian Mackintosh: Agent of Karma
The Man in the Panama Hat
The Rule of Ten — How Prince Andrew Came to Be Exiled to Switzerland
The Soul Exchange
David Lammy on the Run — A Political Comedy Adventure
The Fall and Rise of a Comedy Legend!
Running Clear — How David Defeated Depression

David Lammy Still on the Run
Tripartheid
Unseeable
Zelenskyy
Vladimir Putin: Predestination
The Lord of Purgatory
The Political Lottery — Democracy's Last Best Hope of Survival

Non-Fiction:
How We Will Create Peace in Ukraine and the World
69 Excuses to Drink Alcohol and 1 Reason Not To
The Continuation of the Origin of the Species
Six Ways to Prevent WWIII
Smartphones Are Dumb
Why The British Stopped Breeding
Autistic Jesus
Don't Judge a Book by Its Cover: 21 Remarkable Similarities Between Donald Trump and Tommy Robinson
The List: The Death of Antisocial Behaviour and Noise Pollution — and the Evolution of the Real Estate Industry
Capitalism Hates You
The Internet vs. the Nationalnet
The Far Right and Far Left Are Far from Opposites
10 EASY WAYS Russia Could Destroy Germany and the EU in 2025
The Folly of Colonising the Stars: The Final Nail in the Coffin of AI and Space Colonisation
The Origin of African American Gangsters, Gangs and Ghettos
Five Ways to Create Peace in the Middle East
Make America United Again: The Trump-Harris Co-Presidency 2024 – 2028
How Nigel Farage Became Prime Minister
The Truth at Last! 33 Essential Questions for Conspiracy Theorists
The Truth at Last! 33 Essential Questions for Elon Musk
The Truth at Last! 33 Essential Questions for Prince Harry
The Truth at Last! 33 Essential Questions for Prince Andrew
The Truth at Last! 33 Essential Questions for Tommy Robinson
The Truth at Last! 33 Essential Questions for the Alt-right and Alt-left
The Truth at Last! 33 Essential Questions for Christians
Wokeism Is Crumbs from the Table of Globalist Elites
Why Charles Dickens No Longer Loves the White Working Class
Voluntary Taxation and Capital Punishment: For a Just, Equal and

Corruption-Free Society
Escaping the Cult of Guilt: The Dark Side of Charity and NGOs
Defeating Fentanyl
Ending the Migrant Crisis in Europe: Preventing Class Wars, Race Wars and the Destruction of the EU
Globalisation, Mass Immigration, Wokeism and Multiculturalism on Trial
How Not to Get Sued by J.K. Rowling
One Election Please… How J.K. Rowling Bought British Politics, Hid Her True Self and Hoodwinked the World—an Unauthorised Biographical Exposé
ConjectureMania
The Führer of Asperg: A New Understanding of Fascism, Autism and the Third Reich
Russell Brand: False Prophet
Noise Pollution Kills
The Christ Conspiracy, aka The Rise of the Light Triads
What Is Patriotism?
The M25 Solution — The Creation of the Republic of London
How to Quit Gambling This Week
You Have the Power

www.ingramcontent.com/pod-product-compliance
Lightning Source LLC
Chambersburg PA
CBHW071225260726
48653CB00042B/2501